CASE STUDIES IN
CULTURAL ANTHROPOLOGY

GENERAL EDITORS
George and Louise Spindler
STANFORD UNIVERSITY

———————

THE TWO WORLDS OF THE WASHO
An Indian Tribe of California and Nevada

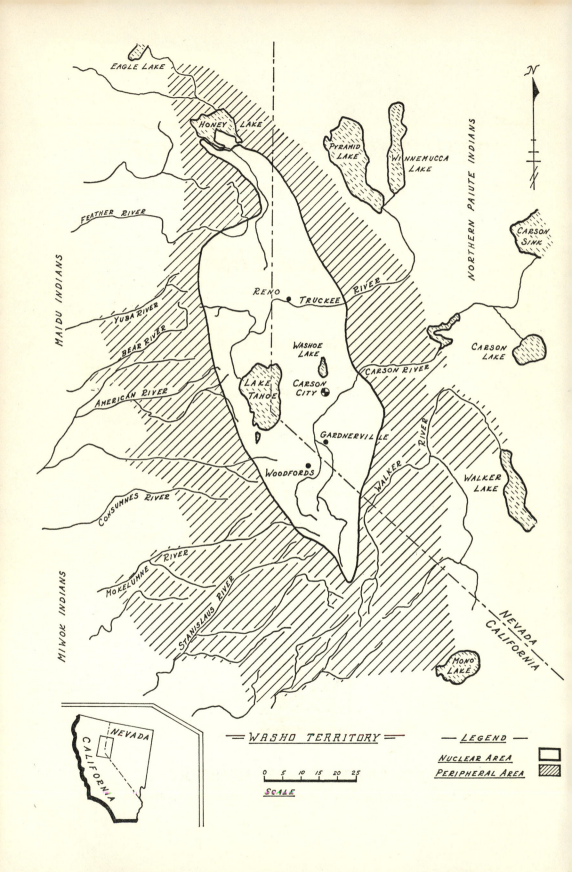

EAGLE LAKE

HONEY LAKE

PYRAMID LAKE

WINNEMUCCA LAKE

NORTHERN PAIUTE INDIANS

CARSON SINK

MAIDU INDIANS

FEATHER RIVER

YUBA RIVER

BEAR RIVER

AMERICAN RIVER

RENO   TRUCKEE   TRUCKEE RIVER

WASHOE LAKE

CARSON RIVER

CARSON LAKE

LAKE TAHOE

CARSON CITY

GARDNERVILLE

WOODFORDS

WALKER RIVER

WALKER LAKE

CONSUMNES RIVER

MIWOK INDIANS

MOKELUMNE RIVER

STANISLAUS RIVER

NEVADA
CALIFORNIA

MONO LAKE

NEVADA

CALIFORNIA

— WASHO TERRITORY —

0 5 10 15 20 25
SCALE

— LEGEND —

NUCLEAR AREA

PERIPHERAL AREA

THE TWO WORLDS OF
THE WASHO

An Indian Tribe
of
California and Nevada

By

JAMES F. DOWNS
The University of Arizona

HOLT, RINEHART AND WINSTON
NEW YORK   CHICAGO   SAN FRANCISCO   TORONTO   LONDON

Picture on cover. A Washo woman weaving an elaborate basket at the turn of the century. *(Photograph courtesy of The Southwest Museum, Los Angeles)*

Foreword

About the Series

These case studies in cultural anthropology are designed to bring to students in the social sciences insights into the richness and complexity of human life as it is lived in different ways and in different places. They are written by men and women who have lived in the societies they write about, and who are professionally trained as observers and interpreters of human behavior. The authors are also teachers, and in writing their books they have kept the students who will read them foremost in their minds. It is our belief that when an understanding of ways of life very different from one's own is gained, abstractions and generalizations about social structure, cultural values, subsistence techniques, and other universal categories of human social behavior become meaningful.

About the Author

Before becoming an anthropologist the author served in the U.S. Navy during World War II and the Korean War, worked as a newsman, professional horseman, and farmer. After conducting field research among the Washo of California and Nevada and the Navajo of Arizona, he received his M.A. and Ph.D. in anthropology at the University of California at Berkeley. He has studied oriental languages and conducted research on Tibetan culture at the University of Washington and has taught at the University of Rochester, the University of Wyoming, and California State College at Los Angeles. He is now an associate professor of anthropology at the University of Arizona.

About the Book

This case study of the Washo Indians of western Nevada and the eastern Sierra slopes of California is one of those rare events in the vast professional literature on the American Indian where a picture of a single tribal culture as a whole is presented. Though Washo culture in its traditional form has virtually ceased to exist at all, its disappearance was gradual enough and its relatively full appearance recent enough so that Professor Downs has been able to put the memories of the older Washo together with known history and knowledge of the culture area to form a coherent and dynamic reconstruction of the traditional Washo way of life. But he never forgets history. There is a sense of time in the book, which is so often lacking in attempts to reconstruct traditional cultures. Even as the traditional patterns of subsistence techniques, of rituals and religion, of kinship and social organization are described, the reader anticipates the dramatic changes in the Washo world to be wrought by the coming of the white man. Each stage of readjustment brought about by this event is analyzed. The Washo are not seen in isolation, but as part of the development of the region and its economy. They interact with and are interdependent with whites in the earlier stages of contact. But then the needs of the white man's economy change and there is no longer any place for most of the Washo. The Washo adapt to this circumstance, as they have adapted to previous conditions. In doing so they exhibit some continuities with the past and their traditional culture and at the same time adopt new patterns of behavior. This is not a happy world for the Washo. For some poverty and uselessness sap their vitality and destroy motivation, but the Washo identity is retained, and the Washo continue to cope with life as it is.

George and Louise Spindler
General Editors

Stanford, California
November 1965

Contents

A Washo family at the turn of the century. The man is erecting a gadu of branches and canvas while the woman dresses her daughter's hair. A tin bucket and iron frying pan have been added to the family's equipment but a woven cradleboard and small carrying basket are still in use. (Courtesy of The Southwest Museum, Los Angeles)

Two Washo women encamped near Lake Tahoe in the late 1890s. White style dress worn in this manner had come to be considered distinctly Washo. The cradleboard was in use as late as 1960. (Courtesy of The Southwest Museum, Los Angeles)

A storage basket made by the famous Washo basket weaver Dah-So-Lah-Lee. For many years she was subsidized by a Nevada physician so that she could devote herself to perfecting her art. Her baskets are among the best in the world and are prized by collectors and museums. (Courtesy of The Southwest Museum, Los Angeles)

The Two Worlds of the Washo

An Indian Tribe of California and Nevada

The Two Worlds of the Washo

Lake Tahoe lies about 6000 feet above sea level in the eastern Sierra Nevada Mountains. The boundaries of the states of California and Nevada join in the center of the lake which has become a great monument to a modern affluent society in which hundreds of thousands of people can spend time and money on leisure activities.

On the southern shore in Nevada where gambling is legal, the view of the lake is blocked by elaborate casinos and night clubs vying with neon signs, fantastic architecture, and the nation's leading entertainers for the attention of the vacationers driving along the highway. Hotels, motels, restaurants, and curio shops crowd each other for space. On the slopes along the lake, real estate developers compete fiercely for land on which to build vacation homes. The California shore, less flamboyant but no less crowded, is lined with vacation homes, summer camps, and lodges. The lake is lashed by the wakes of motor boats and the beaches crowded with funseekers.

Lake Tahoe is the center of a mountain and desert world of recreation. From the tree line above Sacramento, the capital of California, to the glittering casinos of Reno and Carson City, Nevada, the area is devoted to camping, fishing, hunting, skiing, hiking, boating, gambling, and entertainment. To be sure, cattle graze in the mountain meadows and lumbermen work in the forests, but these activities are almost unnoticed in this world of leisure.

Lake Tahoe, however, is the center of another world. The lake was and is the center of a land inhabited by a small and virtually unknown people—the Washo Indians. To their descendants who live almost unnoticed and ignored in a number of "colonies" in the valleys of Nevada east of the lake and on small homesteads in the California mountains, the lake is still the center of the Washo world. These people view the lake as a precious and indeed a sacred spot. In the summer, Washo families frequently visit the lake, not for recreation, but to look at the blue waters and reflect on what they mean. They know that the lake contains the gigantic remains of the Ang, a monster bird which once terrorized their ancestors. They recall the incidents of their own history at each camp-ground, boat dock, and beach where once the Washo camped to fish in the summer. The great rock, towering over the public boat launching is the site of a sacred cave, sanctum of powerful shamans. Each creek flowing into the lake, each stand of trees or outcropping of rocks or lake in the high valleys is associated not only with the secular history of their people but with the sacred myth of the creation of the Washo world. At Emerald Bay, the mischievous companions, the long-tailed weasel and the short-tailed weasel, performed some miracle or committed some misdemeanor. The mysterious and malevolent Water Baby spirit lives in the Carson River, and a monster inhabits a sacred spring near there. In the heights beyond the lake, the dangerous wild men, half man and half demon, still roam. And in a cave above Double Springs the terrible one-legged giant Hanawuiwui lives. A remote meadow is remembered because there an offended shaman worked terrible vengeance against his enemies. In the eyes and hearts of the Washo this is the real world. The vacationers, the casinos, and the flashing speed boats are merely evidence of the latter day intrusions of powerful, numerous, and unknowing strangers. And yet, the Washo must live in this world created by the white man.

This book will describe how the Washo have managed to adjust to the dramatic changes that have occurred in their world in the past century and a half without losing their cultural identity or their contact with their own country. To understand this it will be necessary to examine something of Washo life before these changes occurred. With this understanding we can proceed to analyze the Washo response to the problem of the white man which they have shared with all American Indians.

Anthropologists who study the modern American Indian cannot boast of the romantic aloneness of the pioneering ethnographer reporting for the first time on the lives of some remote and previously unknown people. Instead, we stand on the shoulders of those who have gone before us and share our labors with our contemporaries. The many questions that have been asked of American Indian societies can seldom be answered by a single person. Several generations of anthropologists have studied the American Indian, first reporting the rapidly disappearing cultures of the prereservation times, then turning to documents of history to fill in the gaps in our understanding, and then returning to the modern Indian communities to study the effects of the intrusion of Euro-American culture on their land and their lives. This multifaceted interest in the American Indian has led to the development of specialists. Some students have concerned themselves only with linguistics or, in some cases, only with certain aspects of linguistics. Others have been interested in religion, personality, child-raising practices, economics or intercultural relationships. The list of specific interests is limited only by the imagination of science. One of the areas of widespread interest has been the question of change. How have the various American Indian tribes responded to the presence of another powerful and expansive culture? This study of change in its broadest form has come to be called acculturation. This study of the changes in the life of a small and relatively unknown people can draw then not only on the fieldwork of the author but on over a century of data collected by travelers, government officials, missionaries, and over six decades of specific research by anthropologists.

One of the earliest references to the Washo is to be found in a magazine article printed in 1873. A decade later the famous historian Hubert Howe Bancroft mentions the Washo and recounts a number of their myths, myths which are told today, sometimes in a somewhat altered form, but indesputably reminders of the heritage of the Washo. Since those early references to the Washo, such famous anthropologists as Alfred Kroeber, Samuel Barrett, Edward P. Gifford, and Robert Lowie have studied and reported on various aspects of Washo life. Among later generations of anthropologists such renowned names as Julian Steward, Omar Stewart, E. E. Siskin, and Robert Heizer have appeared in the Washo bibliography. In the past decade a number of younger anthropologists, including the author, have under the inspiration of Warren L. d'Azevedo continued research among these people. In addition to the professionals, a number of dedicated and expert amateurs have made major contributions to our understanding of the Washo. Of these Dr. S. L. Lee and Grace Dangberg are outstanding.

My own field experience among the Washo, a few months in 1959 and several shorter trips in the area in subsequent years, composes only a part of the total fund of knowledge that has been drawn upon to complete this book. A complete bibliography of Washo sources has been published recently and it covers some forty-five pages (d'Azevedo 1964). Many of the people who have contributed to our knowledge of the Washo Indians must of necessity go unmentioned in this book. It is only fair to them and to the reader to indicate the vast amount of labor on the part of many people from which I have been privileged to draw in an attempt to present the following discussion of the changes in the life of the Washo people over the past century.

The Washo inhabited the western edge of a vast area known as the Great Basin and display in a general way a special adjustment to the Basin environment that we can observe from the Sierra Nevada to the Great Salt Lake. Basic to an understanding of the Washo response to the appearance of the white man is an understanding of the adjustment these people had made to their environment. They were people without agriculture, domestic animals, metallurgy, or even a knowledge of pottery making. The tools available to them in exploiting their habitat were simple and few. They also, as we look at the whole history of mankind, were extremely old in a way perhaps representing very little more than the technical capacities of early man. From this base the Washo have been assaulted by the expansive, creative, and enormously technical culture of modern America as it spilled across the continent and at the same time developed and changed from a largely agricultural nation to the largest urban-industrial nation in the world. As the economic development of modern America has turned the sacred lake of the Washo into a gleaming, blinking, and glittering leisure world, so have other developments in American history created situations to which the always adaptable Washo have been forced to adjust. This book will examine the problem of how the Washo have managed to make these adjustments without losing their identity in the process.

2

The Washo

COMPARED TO their nearest neighbors, the Paiute and Shoshone peoples of the Great Basin, the Washo have never been a numerous people. Because their way of life was so generally similar to other Basin peoples, early explorers, when they met Washo bands in western Nevada, seem not to have differentiated them from the other pedestrian hunting and gathering peoples of the area. Even when it became clear that the Washo were not of the same stock as their neighbors, they were seldom encountered, for reasons we shall understand later, in groups larger than a family and, at the most, a few families. Moreover, the Washo often spent the summer months high in the Sierra Nevada, a practice which obscured the true numbers of the population. White observers tended to count only those Indians who were on hand, thus consistently underestimating the tribe. Nonetheless, researches among hunting and gathering peoples throughout the world, particularly groups in arid and semiarid regions, suggest that population density is very low and population seldom rises above the minimum capacity of the environment to support human life. Compared to much of the Great Basin, Washo country was provident and, we can assume, could have supported a larger population. In the middle of the nineteenth century perhaps as many as 3000 speakers of the Washo language lived along the eastern slope of the Sierra Nevada. Some authorities argue that the number was much lower but few would suggest that it was much greater. The Washo seldom, if ever, congregated in a single place. Washo speakers were distributed from the valley of the Walker River in the south to the southern edge of Honey Lake in the north. In general, the Washo remained in a series of valleys at the eastern foot of the Sierra Nevada, wandering both east and west as their search for food directed them but always returning to the gathering and hunting grounds in the lowlands. Each of these valley dwellers were in practice independent of one another, with their own food-taking cycle, their own leaders and their own network of social relations. A common relationship between all Washo speakers was recognized but it carried few obligations with it.

4

It is difficult to draw distinct boundaries when describing the distribution of primitive peoples because the concept of national territory, to be defended on principle because it lies on one side of an imaginary line, is most frequently absent. This is the case with the Washo, who viewed their territory as a series of layers. In the center was Lake Tahoe and the previously mentioned valleys where the Washo fished and hunted and regularly camped. This land was more or less vigorously defended from the intrusions of neighboring Paiute people from Nevada or the Maidu or Miwok to the west. However, even these invasions could be measured in degree. The Washo tended to fight most readily if the strangers sought to fish in "their" lake or hunt "their" large game, such as deer. On the other hand, the Washo seemed to feel the invasion was much less serious if the strangers had simply come to gather plant food. Beyond this central zone was a much wider area in which the Washo wandered on hunting and gathering trips during part of the year. This peripheral zone extended to Walker Lake in the southeast and almost to Pyramid Lake in the northeast. To the west, Washo informants all assert that gathering expeditions went almost to Sacramento, California. Washo hunters pushed into the foothills above the Sacramento Valley, but Washo fishermen were never safe if they attempted to fish in the westward flowing rivers of California. It is certain that if one were interviewing Paiute, Maidu, or Miwok informants the zones described as peripheral Washo would be described as peripheral Paiute or Miwok, and so on. Thus each of these peoples tended to occupy a central area which they defended as their own on certain occasions and returned to as to a home port. But between groups were vaguely defined "grey" zones which were often jointly exploited without undue hostility. It is clear that in the northern and southern extremes of the Washo area Washo bands lived on quite intimate terms with Paiutes in the same area. Such groups were often referred to as "half Paiute" by the Washo living in the central area around the present sites of Carson City, Minden, and Gardnerville, Nevada. To the west, Washo often married into Miwok groups without abandoning their Washo identity.

It should be emphasized that although we speak of Washo movements as "wandering" there was nothing casual or unplanned about these movements. The common view of simple hunting and gathering peoples, or even pastoral nomads, wandering aimlessly over the land in search of food is, as we shall see, quite far from the truth. The exploitation of even a relatively provident environment with such a simple technology required careful planning and a great deal of knowledge about the plants, animals, climate, and soils of the area. However vaguely the boundaries might be defined, it is possible to rather definitely locate the aboriginal Washo country as a lozenge shaped area with Lake Tahoe as a rough center, Honey Lake as the northern extreme, and the headwaters of the Stanislaus River as a southern extreme. Many Indian tribes in the United States have been moved to reservations far removed from their aboriginal grounds or encompassing only a small portion of their original range. The Washo have always lived and continue to live on their home grounds. This is important in understanding how, in spite of enormous changes in their lives, the Washo have remained stubbornly Washo.

Physical Description

The Washo clearly illustrate the fallacy of the still popular belief that there is some meaningful connection between the way of life of a people and the genetic makeup of that people. Beset by a century of dramatic changes, the Washo have remained an identifiable social and cultural unit despite the fact that they have mingled their "blood" with that of many races. The Washo population today carries in its inheritance legacies from all the races which have entered the West as well as that of many if not most of the Indian tribes of the United States. Almost since the earliest period of Indian-white contact, prostitution and common-law and formal marriage have contributed a regular flow of Caucasion genetic material into the population. In addition, Negro individuals frequently have married into the tribe, and many Washo have married or lived with Mexicans. Specific instances of possible oriental parentage have been pointed out by informants. In more recent times, Filipino and even Eskimo genes have entered the Washo genetic heritage. The increased association between Indian groups brought about by the automobile and the Native American Church has led to many intertribal marriages and the integration of schools in both California and Nevada has led to a number of Indian-white marriages. With this mixed genetic history it should be no surprise that there is no single Washo type. For the most part, those people who think of themselves as Washo and are so considered by others display the common features of almost all American Indians. Straight black hair, dark brown eyes, and brown skin are almost universal. Many Washo men and women share characteristics common among the tribes of central California, a kind of robust roundness. Some men may be well over 6 feet and weigh over 200 pounds, and a few women are also large in proportion to their sex. On the other hand, many Washo appear well below average height and some older informants, reportedly "full-blood," are scarcely above 5 feet. Many individuals would be considered to be either Chinese or Japanese were they encountered in the cities of the west coast and many others would pass as Mexicans if they were seen in California. Facial structure tends to a roundness more characteristic of the statuary of early Mexico than the high cheek bones and acquiline noses of the warriors of the Great Plains who serve as the popular model for Indians in this country. Despite the wide variations in physical type, white residents of the area and anthropologists, after a bit of practice, are seldom wrong in identifying the Washo from among the neighboring Paiutes. However, it is more than likely that such observers are responding to a series of subtle and unnoticed cultural clues rather than any distinguishing physical characteristic.

The Language

While genetics or "race" is not a unifying factor among the Washo, the language which they speak has been. Linguistically, the Washo constitute a unique group in the Great Basin. In that vast region, covering all of Nevada and parts of Idaho, Oregon, and Colorado, the languages spoken were all representatives of a language family or stock known as Uto-Aztecan. In this area there were two major divisions, Paiute and Shoshonean.

Shoshonean speakers occupied a broad band extending out of the Basin to the Pacific Ocean. Various dialects and languages of the Uto-Aztecan stock extended south from the Great Basin to the valley of Mexico where the civilized Aztecs spoke a language of this stock, Nahuatl. In the Great Basin the only language not related to Uto-Aztecan was that spoken by the Washo.

For many decades students of American Indian languages, beginning with Leslie Powell who first attempted to classify the languages of North America, listed Washo as a separate language stock with only this single representative in all the world. However, later linguists, continuing the investigations, have decided that Washo is a representative of a widely scattered language stock known as Hokan. Hokan languages are found in California and are spoken by the Esselen, Salinan, and Chumash of the central coast of California. To the north the Achomowi or Pitt-River people of northern California also speaks a Hokan language. These western representatives of the Hokan languages are not closely related to each other, suggesting that the separation into distinct languages occurred many thousands of years ago. There is one school of thought which holds that Hokan speakers are the oldest California population and that subsequent invasions of the west coast have submerged or dispersed the original settlers of the area, leaving only these scattered groups widely separated from each other, each language developing without contact with the other. Another enclave of Hokan languages, even more distantly related, is located in the extreme southern portion of California. Some linguists believe that even more distantly related languages are found far to the east. These people include the Creek, Cherokee, Choctaw, Chickasaw, and Seminole of the southeast and the famous Iroquois of the north. These tenuous relationships should not be considered evidence of anything more than very ancient common stock from which all of these languages must have sprung. Certainly there is no direct relationship between even the Hokan enclaves on the west coast, let alone the eastern representatives of this language family. As this book is being written, linguists are in the field working with Washo speakers attempting to describe the language fully and to further understand its history.

Today all Washo speak English from childhood. The older people speak an "English" that may be difficult for the untrained ear to understand. Perhaps a few younger people no longer understand their language, but the majority of the tribe still speak the language and use it in everyday life. Many of the words used to describe conditions of the past have slipped from their memories. Old people often argue for hours trying to decide for a linguist or an anthropologist whether a certain word means moose or buffalo or elk—all of these species have been extinct (if indeed they ever existed) in this area for well over a hundred years. On the other hand, the language has expanded and developed in order to deal with modern conditions. Washo can discuss such problems as the settlement of the tribe's land claim suit against the government or the problems dealing with white law with only an occasional need to use an English word for which there is no Washo equivalent.

3

The Land

As THE WASHO today live in two cultural worlds, so they have in the past lived in two environmental worlds. The central zone of the Washo homeland lay along the boundary between two life zones. In their quest for food the Washo drew on the resources of three other life zones. The most important area, the strings of valleys lying along the eastern edge of the Sierra Nevada, is part of the region known as the Great Basin. This vast interior area lies to the north of the Colorado River and between the Sierra Nevada on the west and the Rockies to the east. Rivers which rise on the western slope of the Rockies and on the eastern slopes of the Sierra do not drain into the sea but into the center of the Basin. The Great Salt Lake is the largest consequence of this phenomonon known today, but in the past even greater lakes existed in the Basin.

Today the Basin is a high arid area lying in a life zone known to biologists as *Artemisian*. To anyone who has driven through the interior of the United States, the artemisian zones can be recalled as the least inspiring scenery one is apt to encounter. The stark waterless beauty of the true southern desert or the vast almost oceanlike quality of the Great Plains or the spectacular vistas of the mountains provide delights for the eye and the emotions of the traveler. The artemisian zones, however, are remarkable for their unbroken sameness. Sagebrush is the most common plant, growing grey and dull over millions of acres and giving way in the higher reaches of ground to the dull green of greasewood. Rising above these plains are the mountains which form ranges across the entire Basin running generally from north to south. These mountains, rising only a few thousand feet above the already high valleys, are as arid and as uninviting as the valleys. In the higher ranges the stunted, twisted piñon pine grows in great profusion and, as we shall see, greatly affects the life of the Basin peoples. Rivers are few and pitiful in this area. Seldom does a river run year-round, but in the few places where this does happen, an oasis of green marks the central valley floor. Watercourses are often dry for most of the year and then be-

8

come roaring torrents during the season of cloudbursts. They drain into sinks which remain swamps throughout the year or in the lesser sinks they slowly diminish until only a salt-rimmed plate of drying mud remains in midsummer. Springs are small and generally infrequent, and the water table is often extremely deep or in many areas seemingly nonexistent. Extremely detailed hydrographic surveys of recent years have revealed many more natural springs than we had previously suspected, but these are tiny, often dry and of little modern significance, although they may have been important to the Indians of the past.

Wagon train pioneers dreaded the Great Basin perhaps more than any other portion of the trip from east to west. Dry camps were frequent and grazing often sparse or unobtainable. The crossing of the Humboldt sink, some 85 miles of a waterless basin, was a graveyard of pioneer hopes and dreams. It was dotted with the carcasses of oxen, mules, and horses; the wrecks of abandoned wagons; and the treasures of eastern homes thrown away to lighten the load as the travelers struggled to reach water before they and their animals gave out completely. Much of the Great Basin offered little to the white man save for grazing cattle, often at a ratio of 80 or 100 acres per a single head. The stark mountains contain a great many metal and mineral deposits and therefore attracted the most interest in the area. The infrequent well-watered areas became the sites of the small towns of central Nevada; Winnamucca, Battle Mountain, and others.

Despite its formidable appearance, the Basin provided, for those who knew the land and how to exploit it, a surprising amount of food. While the sage and the greasewood provided little more than firewood, the dry earth regularly produced short-lived harvests of seed-bearing grasses of many kinds. Water-holding roots grew underground. The gopher, ground squirrel, and jack rabbit existed in amazing numbers. The pronghorned antelope, although not as numerous as on the Great Plains or in the verdant valleys of California, was common. In the mountains were the desert bighorn sheep. The mule deer was distributed, not thickly, but widely through the area. In addition, numerous edible insects existed, wild fowl came to the sinks and in the higher ranges, the piñon pine provided a singularly plentiful and important staple crop. While the Basin seldom could provide a living for large populations, a small group, energetic and alert to all the possibilities of the area, could survive surprisingly well.

The lowland valleys of the Washo country were perhaps the best of all the Basin environments. Compared to the waterless and frequently rainless steppes to the east they were well watered with rains falling in the winter and spring and occasionally in summer cloudbursts. The larger watercourses such as the Carson and Walker rivers flowed during the entire year. Each of these valleys repeated the general Great Basin pattern. Streams and rivers flowed east out of the Sierra Nevada into lakes and sinks in the low portion of each valley. Aside from the green belts along the rivers and the luxuriant growth of the sinks, the land was covered with the dull sagecovered plant life of the Basin steppes, giving way to greasewood and finally to the dark green of the piñon forests. Antelope and jack rabbit lived in the valleys. Deer were to be found in the foothills to the east and west. Waterfowl flocked to the sinks, and wild fowl such as sage hen were numerous. In addition, ground squirrels, gophers, and field mice were especially plentiful. As attractive as the land was, in comparison to the bone dry steppes to the east, the Washo country was not a benign habitat. Winters were cold with snowfall a regular occurrence. Freezing temperatures were common in the winter, and severe floods in the late winter and spring turned the valleys into quagmires. After the brief blooming of the spring, the valleys became dry very quickly, save along the margins of the watercourses. Summer heat was often intense, remaining in the 90s for long periods and frequently soaring well above 100° F. The more mobile game tended to drift out of the hot basins and into the higher country. As this occurred, many Washo turned to the other half of their physical world, the high mountains to the west. The Artemisian zone of the eastern valleys is at an altitude of from 3000 to almost 5000 feet. The transition to the *Sierran* zone is abrupt. The mountains rise directly out of the floor of the valleys without intervening foothills. The great eastern escarpment of the Sierra soars to 8000 and 10,000 feet above the valley floor. The sheer mountain sides are covered with pine and cedar, and are in many places virtually impossible to traverse. Entry into the mountain world from the valleys was by way of a number of passes. Many of these are the sites of today's modern highways as they were in the past the routes of immigrant wagons. Others, too high and tortuous for either wagon or automobile, are even today little more than trails. The major passes such as Carson, Ebbets, Donner, Monitor, Beckwith, and Walker have played important roles in the history of the modern west. In many cases the pass is linked to the lower valleys by the dramatic canyon of a large river such as the Carson or the Truckee.

Once over the eastern escarpment the mountains fall off into a series of high valleys from 6000 to 8000 feet above sea level. The largest of these valleys is the site of Lake Tahoe, some 30 miles long and 10 miles wide. In addition, there are dozens of other high mountain lakes and hundreds of streams watering this high country. Damp mountain meadows abound amid the pine-covered slopes. The mountain world provided an entirely different set of resources for the Washo. Although the lowland rivers provided some fishing, it was the high country to which the Washo turned for this all important food. Deer were common throughout the mountains, and mountain bighorns in the higher peaks. The woodchuck and a number of species of squirrel were numerous. Fur bearers such as the fox, lynx, bobcat, mink, beaver, and weasel were taken in the mountains. On the highest peaks eagles, prized for their magical feathers, nested. The damp mountain earth provided a wide variety of root and bulb plants and a number of greens and berries in the summer, and as the millions of vacationers have learned, the temperature is never uncomfortably high. There was always an adequate water supply and plenty of food. Firewood and shelter were easily obtainable. However, in the high country winter came early, with the first snows falling in October, and stayed late, with some of the valleys snowbound in May and early June. The winters were severe. The land was covered many feet deep with snow, and lakes and streams were frozen. Game animals either went into hibernation or drifted into the lowlands. In ancient times it is doubtful that any Washo remained in the mountains in the winter. The problem of survival in such an environment was quite beyond the capabilities of a people with such a simple technology.

Above the high valleys the mountains provided yet two more life zones from which the Washo could draw sustenance, although they seldom dwelt there. Above the lakes are the high *Alpine* plateaus where pine gives way to green and silver aspen groves set in wide grassy meadows. Deer often inhabited this area and a number of smaller game animals as well, but this zone provided little else. Above this rose the barren rocky peaks of the *Arctic* zone above timber line. The plant life in this area is limited to some grasses, mosses, and lichens, and in the lower reaches, a few hardy trees. The mountain sheep roamed here and the often fat marmot, but in general the extremely high country offered little. Beyond the ridge of the Sierra the mountains fall away for nearly a hundred miles in ever-descending steps until in the foothills the pines give way to the oak-dotted grasslands typical of much of interior California. This zone was seldom a permanent home for the Washo, but it was often visited in order to collect acorns, which were exceedingly plentiful and exceedingly nutritious. Here too the deer population was high when compared to Nevada. In the summer and fall the weather is hot and dry, but the winters are comparatively mild and a few Washo families sometimes wintered there rather than risk being trapped by the snows in the mountains by attempting to return across the mountain too late in the fall.

Thus, the Washo were able to draw on the resources of three main types of country: the arid but botanically and zoologically varied land east of the mountains, the plentiful fish, game, and plant life of the high mountains; and finally the animal and plant life of the western slopes of the mountains. A list of all the plants used by the Washo for food and all the species of animals hunted would be far too long to publish here. An indication of the potential of this land can be found in the estimate made by one zoologist that on an average every square mile of Nevada contained a population of nearly 12,000 mammals of all species. Of course most of these animals were small—squirrels, gophers, and field mice—but even such small animals in the aggregate suggest a great potential for those willing to seek out and find them. The Washo country is the only part of Nevada in which a number of animals, including the bear and several other fur bearers, still exist.

In this section we have seen a very general picture of the stage on which the Washo worked out their way of life. It has been estimated that the tribe regularly occupied some 13,000 square miles of this country. This means that even if we accept the highest estimate of population, the human density in the area was only a fraction over four persons per square mile. This was among the higher density ratios for the Great Basin but not as high as some. It was, however, enormously higher than the ratio of two and a half square miles per person reported for Central Nevada.

4

Using the Land

THE FAMOUS ANTHROPOLOGIST A. L. Kroeber once listed the Washo as
among the simplest cultures on the North American continent. Without
agriculture or domestication and with an extremely simple technology
such societies are heavily influenced by the quest for food. Although the Washo
habitat was more benign than that of other Basin societies, it could provide adequate support for the tribe only if it was most carefully exploited. In large part,
Washo society and Washo social behavior were shaped by the environment. One
might say that the Washo, in the absence of a complex technology, used their
social structure as a tool in exploiting their environment. In this section we will
examine the actual business of making a living under these conditions and see
how the institutions of Washo society served to most efficiently exploit the land.

The Washo obtained food by three means: gathering, fishing, and hunting. Each of these activities required knowledge and skills and could be most
successfully carried out by groups composed in a certain way. No single means
of livelihood could provide a year-round supply of food for these people. Their
situation and that of the majority of people of the Great Basin was one in
which the failure of any of the varied sources of sustenance could spell disaster.
Far to the northwest an elaborate nonagricultural culture was developed by the
coastal peoples who were able to depend almost solely on the endless supply of
fish. On the Great Plains, the introduction of the horse and the great numbers
of buffalo made possible the development of a vigorous and elaborate hunting
culture. Over much of California the infinite supply of acorns served as a basis
for large and relatively elaborate societies. But in the Basin, no matter how
plentiful any given source of food might be, it would not support a population
for an entire year. Therefore, the movements of the Washo people and even the
organization of the family life were at least partially shaped by the exploitive
possibilities of the environment. The Washo "calendar" might be said to be divided into three years: the fishing year, the gathering year, and the hunting year.

The Fishing Year

The year began for the Washo in hunger. The last of the seeds and meat taken in the fall were usually consumed by the end of the winter and the weeks before spring were a time of near starvation. Hunting was seldom good at this time and gathering even less so. Late winter was a time of death, for the very young and the very old. The early weeks of spring provided fresh food in the form of bulb plants and early grasses, and spring was a prelude to the season of plenty provided by the upland lakes. As soon as the snows began to leave the lower foothills young men and boys, often accompanied by young unmarried women, began to trek into the mountains. Before the snow had left its shores these young people arrived at Lake Tahoe. There they lived in caves and other natural shelters. Wearing only loin cloths and small aprons and protected from the still cold spring weather by rabbit skin blankets, they began to fish for whitefish. This early trek of the youths relieved the pressure on what little food remained available to the older people and children in the lowlands. In some cases, the young men would return to the winter camp with fish so that their families might have enough food to survive and to regain their strength for their own trek to the lake. Relieved of the continual threat of starvation that was part of the winter, on their own and away from their elders and free of the restrictions that winter placed on their movements, the young people treated these expeditions as adventures. Young men displayed their hardiness by entering the tributary streams with fish harpoons, although the water could have been only a few degrees above freezing. With plenty of food, there was time for social get-togethers between people from different parts of the Washo country. A form of field hockey was popular as were archery contests and races. Dancing was common and the presence of young women provided an opportunity for courtship and sexual relations. In addition to fishing, the woodchucks provided meat, albeit thin and not too nourishing after a winter's hibernation. Early spring plants provided much needed vegetable food. But the primary activity was taking the whitefish, which broiled on a stick was eaten while fresh in great quantity. The fish were also dried in the open air for future use.

As the weather improved, the people remaining in the lowlands began to move toward the lake. Each family decided for itself when to leave the winter camp and move. Families composed of younger and more vigorous people began earliest. Groups with old people and infants tended to wait until the weather was better before moving to the 6000 foot elevation of Lake Tahoe. By early June almost the entire Washo population was encamped on the shores of the lake. As we shall see later, the Washo tribe was rather vaguely divided into territorial groups. This division was adhered to in the spring migration, with the people from Sierra Valley and Honey Lake making camp on the north edge of the lake while the people from Carson Valley, Woodfords, and the southern portion of the Washo country camping to the south.

By early June, many species of fish began to swim out of the deep lake into the streams in order to spawn. The two most important species were native trout and a type of large sucker which came up the streams by the thousands, their bodies crowded from bank to bank. Informants recall that their older relatives told them of the times before the appearance of the white man when the spawning runs were accompanied with religious ritual, although its exact form has now been forgotten. A number of accounts suggest that certain men would dream that the run would start soon and would advise the people to be prepared. This waiting period was a time of dancing and singing when respected elders would exhort the people to obey the laws of the Washo and to live properly. There may have been some ritual attached to the taking of the first fish. The tribes to the west often had elaborate first fish ceremonies. Among the Washo, such ritual seems not to have been elaborate nor important and it was quickly abandoned as the whites appeared in the Lake Tahoe country. It may have been that only certain groups practiced such ritual at all inasmuch as it is most frequently mentioned in connection with the northern bands.

The actual spawning runs were time of intense activity. Men, women, and children from the oldest to the youngest assisted in gathering as many fish as possible from the hordes struggling up stream. Taking fish under these conditions required little skill. People waded into the streams armed with baskets, scooping up the fish and tossing them onto the bank. There the fish were taken up and boned, split down the back and the spine and ribs removed, leaving two meaty fillets. These were placed on racks to dry in the sun and air. Female fish were stripped of their roe which was eaten raw or spread out to dry to be stored against future need. And, of course, fresh fish was broiled and eaten regularly. Often, fishing at the height of the run continued through the night by torchlight, which reflected on the backs of the fish enough to allow the fishermen and women to work. The spawning runs lasted perhaps two weeks during which time enormous amounts of fish were prepared. The leading authority on the native fish of America reports that this area could produce, on a year-round basis, as much as 200 pounds of fish per square mile. However, Washo technology was not able to take full advantage of this resource. The Washo knew of no other way to preserve fish save to spread the fillets on a rack exposed to the sun and air. This method would keep the flesh edible for a long period in the high cool mountain country. However, the Washo had learned that if the dried fish were taken into the warm lowlands it would spoil. A knowledge of smoking, as was practiced on the northern coast, would perhaps have enabled the Washo to live nearly year-round on the resources of Lake Tahoe and its contributing streams. However, without this knowledge, the fish resources were useful only while the Washo remained in the high country.

As the summer progressed, the snow left the higher valleys which were the sites of many other smaller lakes. When the spawning runs began to decline, individual families began to leave their lakeside camps and head into the higher mountains. This was done with some reluctance because the spring fishing period was a time of much social interaction. Relatives and friends separated during the winters, renewed acquaintances. Leaders of the various groups met and conferred. Medicine men competed with each other in displays of their magical powers. Dances and games were held. Courtships were initiated or re-

newed and marriages consummated. News about the presence of game, the pros-
pects for the gathering of seeds and other vegetable food, and the behavior of
the neighboring tribes was exchanged. Above all, it was a period when the
Washo, often scattered and isolated, were joined as a single people engaged in
the same activities. From Lake Tahoe, families and groups of families went to
Tallac and Blue Lake and dispersed throughout the mountain country where
they set up camps for the summer. The damp mountain meadows provided an
increasing amount of vegetable food. The animal life of the mountains became
more available for hunters. At Blue Lake every spring and summer great numbers of mountain quail, decoyed by the reflections on the water, were found
drowned. These were regularly gathered to add to the larder of the people who
camped there. The high mountain camps are still identifiable because of the
presence of granite boulders pock-marked with bedrock mortars, or *lam,* where
the Washo women sat during the day to grind seeds or berries or to pulverize
dried fish eggs. While the women gathered and prepared vegetable food, the
men fished the lakes and streams. In the absence of the spawning runs, fishing
was a business calling for a great deal of skill. The best fishermen often used a
two-pronged fish spear. The head was made separately of wood, sinew, and
bone, and fitted onto a pole. Fish could be taken with a spear by a man standing
on the bank or rock overlooking a river or stream. Frequently, fishermen stood
waist deep in the water, alert to the flash of a fish swimming nearby. Because of
the deflection caused by the water, skill with a harpoon was hard won, coming
only after long years of practice. Platforms were built over good fishing spots so
that the fisherman could take fish with a spear or with a net. Dip nets wielded
by a single man were woven of plant fibers. Larger nets were handled by several
men at once, working either from the banks or wading in the water. The Washo
also made rather elaborate bone hooks with which they caught fish from deep
pools or in the lakes. In addition to these active means of taking fish, the
Washo often diverted small streams so that they could gather the fish stranded
by the receding water or trapped in shallow pools. Sometimes, in rapid streams
where fish were difficult to see, dams were built to pond the water so that a man
with a net, spear or hook could see his quarry. In the absence of a net, a gathering basket might be wielded as a net and frequently willow wands were woven
into a fish trap. These traps, completely blocking a stream, were the property of
a single man or family. Fish wiers and dams were also constructed to enable
fishermen with specially made conical baskets to wade into the water after their
quarry. For bait, the Washo gathered angleworms, salmon eggs, and minnows.
As the summer went on, the Washo began to drift toward the lowlands. Some
families started the trip as soon as the fishing at Lake Tahoe dropped off, making their summer camps along the banks of the upper reaches of the Carson or
the Truckee rivers rather than at the high lakes. As the water level began to
drop in the heat of the summer, minnows would be taken from shallow pools in
flat-seed winnowing baskets. Hundreds of the tiny fish were taken at a time and
baked in an earth oven. This was a hole in the ground in which a fire had
burned for several hours. The fire was scraped out, the minnows put in the hole

and covered with earth, and another fire built on top of the hole. This method of cooking minnows disappeared soon after the Washo obtained frying pans from the whites.

The trek to the lowlands was not motivated by fish resources. In fact, by late summer, fishing was not good enough to supply all the food needed. The important issue, however, was the fact that the many different grasses of the valleys were ripening and the seed harvest was at hand. Interest in fishing waned as the gathering season approached. The fall was also the time of the most intense hunting of big game so that fishing became a secondary activity. However, it was never completely abandoned. Even in the depth of winter, when no other food was available, it was possible to fish. The ice on deep pools could be broken open and fish taken with hook and line or by spearing, or nets could be spread between two holes and the fish trapped in them. Minnows crowded into pockets in the frozen streams were also easy to catch. Thus, the fishing year lasted all year long with its peak in the early spring and its importance slowly tapering off until the following spring.

Fishing Technology, Society, and Culture

The fish resources of the Washo country were comparatively high. They were at their highest at a crucial time in the food gathering cycle. At the end of the winter when food was scarce, the spawning runs at Lake Tahoe provided an enormous amount of food for a relatively low expenditure of energy. From this high point, the return from fishing dropped until it became easier and more profitable to turn to other sources of food. However, throughout the entire year, fish provided the Washo with some and, at times, their only food. To obtain this important part of their diet, the Washo developed the most complex part of their technology. Compared to hunting and gathering, fishing required immeasurably more tools and devices and an exceedingly high degree of skill. The making of fishhooks and spears was a complex job, equal to the making of bows and arrows, and their use required as much practice. Fish weirs, dams, traps, and fishing platforms were all projects much more ambitious and complex than even the Washo winter house, or *galesdangl*. The Washo skill at basketry was employed in fishing as was the knowledge of string and rope making from vegetable fibers. We have seen, however, that technology failed them in the matter of preserving enough fish to last the year round. This failure profoundly affected the yearly cycle and the social organization of the Washo. Fishing was important socially because it tended to concentrate population. The most marked example is at Lake Tahoe where almost all the Washo people gathered in the spring. Perhaps at no other time of the year did all the Washo come together for so long a time. It is not surprising then that the lake plays an important role in Washo culture. It is the center of the Washo world, geographically and socially. Washo mythology and folklore centers around the lake. Even today, almost every bay, inlet, and stream mouth has a legendary or mythological association. On the shores of the lake grew the dangerous and semisacred wild parsnips. From the great rock where the shamans had a secret hiding place to the other end of the lake there is, according to Washo belief, a roadway of white sand on which a powerful shaman could walk without drowning. And, as we shall see, it was the lake and its environs which the Washo defended most vigorously against intruders.

However, fishing is an activity which does not require large-scale cooperation. One needs only to look at a modern trout stream or fishing pier to realize the truth of this statement. Each fisherman searches the same water, using the same methods, but each is lost in his own isolation. In a sense this was true of the Washo. Even during the spawning runs, each family fished for itself. The number of fish was so great that there was little competition. There was more than plenty for all. When fishing by other methods, a single man or, at the most, a few men could perform all the necessary tasks. A platform could be made by a man and his sons or brothers. A half dozen men, the males of a single big family or two average families, could build a fish trap or dam or divert a stream. A stream only a few yards wide could be swept by three or four men holding a net or pushing a bundle of willows to entrap the fish. There was no particular advantage to large-scale cooperation. If Washo technology had included the ability to build boats sturdy enough for long-line fishing on Lake Tahoe, perhaps institutions based on the necessary cooperation would have been developed. The Washo knew only of boats made of bundles of tule which were useful on shallow lakes. Fishing encouraged association, at Lake Tahoe and the lesser lakes of the mountains and along the banks of the streams and rivers, but it did not encourage organization. A man and his wife and children, with a few unmarried relatives, could catch all the fish they could use. Once again we can speculate about the development of more complex social institutions based on fishing had the Washo been able to maintain themselves year round on fish resources. But, as we have seen, this was not possible and we will see how the demands of gathering and hunting worked to prevent any further development of a more complex organization.

The Gathering Year

While fishing started at a high point, producing a large amount of food at a time when it was badly needed and tending to concentrate people after a period of winter isolation, gathering was quite the opposite. The amount and varieties of plant food available to the Washo in the several environmental zones they inhabited was almost infinite. But seldom was it available in large amounts in a single place. Moreover, it was available in the smallest amounts and in the most widely dispersed places in the spring. During the winter little vegetable food was available. Water cress grew all winter long in some streams and it was eaten by those who found it, but most winter vegetable food was limited to that which had been gathered and stored in the summer and fall. By spring, the Washo had been living on pine nut flour, grass seeds, and dried meat for several months with very little green food or fresh meat. Usually by spring the food stored against the winter was gone, or very nearly so. The gathering year began with the first appearance of early plants. Wild lettuce and wild spinach were gathered in the foothills as soon as the leaves appeared. These plants seldom occurred in large beds so that some people were lucky and others were not. For people camped in the foothills, particularly to the east near the piñon groves, there were crops of what are called wild potatoes and Indian sweet potatoes. But once again, these did not occur in large amounts or in heavy concentration. People who lived near such beds gathered and cooked the tubers but there was never enough to encourage people to gather and search for them. In the lower reaches of the valleys there were many small bulbous plants. These were an important source of food in the springtime, but they were usually dug up and eaten on the spot by whoever found them. There were never enough in one place to justify gathering them for the family to consume. Near the swamps and sinks, and particularly near the hot springs which dot the eastern edge of the Sierra, the new shoots of the tule were gathered and the roots were frequently pulled up and cooked. Gathering in the spring was a hand-to-mouth-activity, important because it supplied fresh food when it was badly needed in the Washo diet. Perhaps in bad years it staved off starvation. But it was only a temporary source of food for families headed toward Lake Tahoe or an adjunct to the spring diet of fish during the gathering at the lake.

As the summer progressed and the tribe began to disperse, the tempo of gathering picked up. While the men fished the lakes and streams, the women spent more and more of their days wandering in the mountain meadows or in the foothills gathering plant food. Their only tools were a digging stick and a burden basket. The plants gathered depended on the spot where the camp was located and the season. Some plant foods were available for only a few days or weeks. During the summer, the mountains produced a variety of plants but none of them in quantity sufficient to overshadow the importance of fishing. In the early summer, the high meadows produced a native sunflower from which the seeds could be stripped and ground into flour. Wherever there was a damp meadow or swamp, the common cattail offered roots, new shoots, and seeds. In the early part of the summer before the fluffy cattail was formed, the seeds were wrapped in leaves and placed in the fire. They cooked into a brown paste which was eaten like candy and considered a singular treat. The sap of the sugar pine was another confection. The sap balls were picked from the bark and chewed by children and adults. During July, the wild strawberry plants bloomed around Lake Tahoe. Later in the summer they appeared at the higher elevations and were picked wherever found to be eaten fresh or mashed into a juice to form a sweet drink. From the spring on through the summer wild onions grew in profusion throughout the high country and were eaten raw with meals. The gooseberry was gathered in the late summer, but the Washo had no way of preserving them so that they were eaten only while blooming. The damp places of the mountains also produced wild rhubarb which was eaten fresh and cooked and was often dried to be eaten later. In the brief period it was available, many people went into the mountains to gather as much as they could carry against the winter food shortages. A number of root plants and bulbs called by various names, turnips, potatoes, and so on were found in large amounts in the mountains and formed the greater part of the Washo diet during the summer, although once again they were not preserved.

As the summer lengthened and productivity of fishing began to drop, gathering became more and more important. Most of the people camped in the mountains began to trek into the valleys east of the Sierra. Usually a few families would head west toward the foothills overlooking the Sacramento Valley. There they would gather chokecherries and wild grass seeds and hunt deer while waiting for the ripening of the acorns. Some of these people would return before the snows, but every year a few Washo families would remain on the western side of the mountain wintering alone or moving into Miwok villages to wait for the spring when they would go east to join their fellow tribesmen at Lake Tahoe. For those who went east into Nevada, the late summer and fall were periods of much movement. The usefulness of plant foods depended on the ability of a family to take advantage of opportunities as they occurred. While some species of plants were widely distributed in the lowlands, they seldom were ripe at the same time. Grass seeds might be ready for harvest in one place while they were still green only a few miles away. Thus, to take advantage of the many plants, the Washo had to be almost continually on the move. A few days of picking in one area would exhaust the supply and then the family would have to move on to another spot.

The irregularity of summer harvest and the limited areas in which plants ready for collecting occurred led to a wide dispersal of population and frequent movements. During this period, the Washo lived without housing, often simply camping without shelter at a suitable location or throwing up a windbreak of brush called a *gadu*. The summer was also a period when especially desirable crops led families to undertake long journeys. The report of a plentiful supply of chokecherries would lead many families to travel 20 or 30 miles to gather them. Good harvests of buckberry were common around the present site of Topaz, on the California-Nevada line. These berries were gathered in great number and dried for the winter. The various plants, combined with the more than adequate number of fish available, made summer a time of plenty, although to take advantage of the food supply the Washo had to move often. A drought could, of course, reduce the supply of plant food, but seldom would a situation develop wherein none of the many dozens of varieties of berries, roots, grasses, and seeds were not available. A short supply, while it might not lead to summer starvation, boded ill for the winter. The summer was important for the amount of surplus food over daily needs that could be saved against the winter. Seeds— wild mustard—pigweed, saltbrush, rabbitbrush, sand grass, and many others were particularly prized because they stored so well. Fruit which could not be stored was eaten on the spot in great quantity in order to preserve the grass seeds for periods of scarcity. The large number of chokecherries consumed in the summer are credited by the Washo for the presence of clumps of this tree throughout their land. The discarded pits, they claim, grew into small groves of trees which mark the sites of old camp grounds. The tempo of gathering against winter famine increased in late summer. During this period, the seed plants matured and were ready for harvesting. When this occurred it was a race against time to collect as much as possible before the seeds were disgorged for natural reseeding. And, as we have seen, the harvesting period varied greatly from place to place. To gather an adequate supply of seeds, Washo families were almost constantly on the move at this time, racing to collect as many seeds as possible.

As the season progressed from late summer to early fall, the attention of the Washo shifted more and more toward the culmination of the gathering year, the piñon harvest. As provident as the valleys and foothills might be, the supplies of the summer would not have lasted through the early winter. The piñon pine was the answer not only for the Washo but for almost all the people of the Great Basin. By late fall the widely scattered Washo people were beginning to converge once again. This time the direction of the trek was to the east to the range of low mountains where the pinon pine grew. Unlike Lake Tahoe, the piñon groves were relatively widely disbursed and the piñon gathering period did not lead to the assembly of all the Washo. The northern bands tended to concentrate in the hills north and slightly west of Reno, Nevada. The southern bands converged on an area to the south and east of Minden and Gardnerville, Nevada. Unlike the spring trek to the lake, the Washo were not on the verge of starvation in the fall. Plant food was plentiful, game was available, the people were well fed and healthy. This was a time of celebration and ritual in preparation for the piñon harvest.

The piñon pine bears a big cone containing many dozens of extremely large meaty seeds commonly called pine nuts. Unlike the sticky cones on many other pines, the piñon cone gives up its seeds relatively easily. These seeds could be gathered in large amounts between the time of ripening and the time they were expelled onto the ground. It was this harvest which provided the staple food of Washo life. In two weeks or a month the Washo could collect enough seeds to provide a basic food through most of the winter. The piñon harvest was regular for the country as a whole, but sometimes the trees in a specific area would bear few, if any, nuts. Thus, even in this instance gathering required that the Washo be able to shift ground, seek a new gathering spot, or some other alternative. However, there were many groves and even the most industrious Washo seldom could gather all the nuts available. The unfortunate who found that his customary grove did not provide enough food for winter could usually find picking rights somewhere else. By early October thousands, perhaps tens of thousands, of pounds of piñon nuts had been gathered and prepared for winter storage. The gathering year was for all practical purposes finished. Save for those families which maintained winter camps near the piñon groves, the people began to drift west again. Along the foothills and in particularly desirable spots in the valleys they set up winter camps and began to collect firewood, making great piles, higher than their winter houses, against the deep snows and bitter weather.

We see that the gathering year was much shorter than the fishing year. It began slowly with the earliest appearance of plants in the spring and grew in importance as more and more plants became available. Toward the end of the summer, the Washo people were involved in an almost frenzied gathering round until the final culmination of the gathering year in the piñon nut harvest. If the summer was good and the piñon pines fruitful, starvation could be avoided.

Plants and the Pattern of Washo Life

Although the gathering year began slowly and lasted only through the growing months of the plant life of the region, gathering permeated every phase of Washo life. During this period from spring to fall, vegetable foods played an increasingly important role in supplying food. And, in the final phase of the gathering year, the piñon harvest spelled the difference between security and starvation in the winter. The technology of fishing is immeasurably more complex than that of gathering, requiring as it does the making of many fishing devices and the fishing skills to make use of those devices. The gatherer requires only a digging stick to probe for roots and bulbs and baskets in which to carry the harvest. And once learned, the skills of harvesting are relatively simple. But to be an efficient gatherer requires a vast fund of knowledge about the growth cycle of dozens of plant species, an understanding of the effect of weather on growth and knowledge of soils and growing conditions. These mental skills can be taught in part. Many of them required learning through experience, so it was the oldest of the Washo women who were the most expert gatherers. Except for the pine nut and those foods taken in small amount and eaten on the spot, all gathering was done by the women. Perhaps more than any other aspect of Washo economic life, gathering gave continuity to the Washo year. Fishing and, as we shall see, hunting tended to supply foods in large amount over relatively short periods. Gathering supplied food over a longer period. It also provided the link between the plenty of the summer and the following spring when plenty came again. Fishing could be done in specific areas or not at all. Animals tended to frequent the same zones or to be absent. However, plant life would flourish in one place in one year and somewhere else in the next. A knowledge of the hows and whys of plant growth and native understanding of the relationship between spring rains and fall harvests is an important element in the Washo understanding of his universe. It might be said that fishing and hunting were arts but gathering approached a primitive applied science.

The preparation of plants differed radically from either fish or game. The latter could be air dried and later ground to be boiled, or it could be broiled or roasted fresh to be eaten on the spot. One needed to know how to butcher but little else. Plants, however, required treatment before they were palatable or even digestible. Wild spinach had to be leached by being soaked in a rapidly moving stream, otherwise the cooked greens would be too bitter to eat. Most plant seeds had first to be husked and separated from their chaff, an operation for which special winnowing baskets were made. Most seed plants required cooking of some sort before they were digestible. Washo women knew how to parch seeds with coals in special baskets and then grind them into flour, which would keep for many months. The piñon nut, rich and oily, will not keep long in a freshly picked state. Several different methods of precooking the nuts were practiced in order to keep them for a long period. The acorn had to be hulled, ground into flour, and the tannic acid leached out of the meal. This was usually accomplished by placing the meal in a shallow pit in the sand and pouring warm water through it. The grinding was accomplished in a *lam,* or bedrock mortar, using an elongated stone pestle. Other seeds were ground on a *demge,* a flat stone similar to a Mexican *metate* save for the legs. These were carried from place to place when camp was moved.

The structure of Washo society reflects the influence of gathering. It has been demonstrated that in gathering operations of this nature cooperation is of no assistance in increasing the harvest. Ten women gathering wild mustard can collect no more per capita than one woman. In fact, the group distracted by gossip, may actually collect less per capita. Thus, there was little encouragement for large groups to form even in an area of luxuriant growth. Each family would gather for its own. At times, with crops which appeared in small plots, only small groups could take advantage of the plants. A large group would simply exhaust the supply but no one would get enough, whereas a single family or small group could exploit a small patch of seeds and completely support itself for a few days at least. Even during the piñon harvest, cooperation of groups any larger than the family was unnecessary. Therefore, while piñon harvest was sufficient to encourage larger gatherings for ritual and recreation, it did not support the development of larger institutionalized groups. Once the crop was exploited the families dispersed, each pursuing its own destiny. There was very little ritual connected with gathering. No one dreamed of plant harvests as men are said to have dreamed of spawning runs. No one had to observe taboos prior to gathering, as we shall see was so common in hunting. No women are reported to have had special magical powers to increase their gathering ability, as did all good hunters. There was a taboo against breaking the limbs of the piñon tree, but this was a practical conservation measure despite the semisacred nature of the taboo. A man could, if he feared that there would not be rain enough for a good harvest, soak an old piñon cone in water and leave it in a nearby grove. All in all, gathering was a much more mundane and rational activity than either hunting or fishing. However, the piñon harvest was an occasion of the largest ritual of the Washo people. These gatherings, mentioned earlier, were called *gumsaba,* usually translated by the Washo as "big time."

The Big Time

The early fall was a time when the three phases of Washo subsistence activity coincided and if the year had been good it was a time of plenty. Fishing had not dropped off in the lower streams and rivers, game animals were at their best at this time, the various grass seeds and berries were harvested and the piñon nut harvest was ready. And unlike the spring, when the people were suffering from a shortage of food if not outright starvation, the population was

relatively well fed from a spring of fishing and a summer of gathering. This
was a time when large numbers of Washo could come together with the assurance that there was food enough for all. A well fed population was ready physically and spiritually for ritual activities and games. Moreover, after a summer of
constant movement and relative isolation they were anxious for a period of social interaction, of story telling, courtship, gossip, and good fellowship.

In the distant past it is probable that the Washo in various parts of the
country held separate *gumsaba* near their gathering grounds. However, most
Washo today remember the *gumsaba* which were held in the latter part of the
nineteenth and early part of the twentieth centuries and these have come to be a
model upon which modern descriptions are based. The most popular gathering
place was a small valley amid the piñon groves known as Double Springs Flats.
Toward the end of the summer families and bands began to gravitate toward
this spot. As the piñon harvest neared, most of the tribe had set up camp in a
large circle, the people from various sections of the Washo country camping together in specific segments of the circle. Some informants recall that an
influential leader in the area would have a dream calling the meeting together
and would send a messenger throughout the area with a rawhide string on
which the number of knots indicated the number of days before the meeting.
Each day the messenger untied a knot. As the people gathered, the men set out
to hunt. Some informants reported that the hunting continued over a four-day
period. Throughout the United States four was a mystic number in Indian life.

While the men hunted, the women began to gather piñon nuts and other
vegetable food. Each day before they began gathering they took a ritual bath.
During the four-day period the leader who had called the meeting fasted, drink-
ing only cold water and eating small amounts of cooked pinon nuts. During his
fast he prayed for the success of the piñon harvest and good luck for the hunters. Each night the people danced the shuffling and monotonous round dance,
which served the Washo in all ritual and social occasions. Gambling games were
staged between teams and in the daytime races were held with the winners receiving food and deerskins. Teams representing the various sections of Washo
country played a form of hockey. At the end of four days, according to the accounts given by old people, the food gathered and hunted was pooled and a respected elder chosen to divide it equitably. Each family head received enough to
feed his family. During the feast which followed, respected leaders prayed and
exhorted the people to behave properly, to avoid marital strife and hostile actions toward other Washo, and to be hospitable and kind. At the end of the
feast the people all took a ritual bath. At Double Springs Flats they used baskets
to dip water from the springs. If the *gumsaba* was held near a river, the crowd
of men, women, and children went there to bathe. After the ceremony, the
Washo were free to disperse into the piñon groves for the real harvest. Most
anthropologists who have worked with the Washo agree that the foregoing de-
scription is highly idealized. Washo culture appears singularly without rigid
rules specifying time and place for group activities. Given the need to take advantage of whatever hunting, fishing, or gathering opportunity occurred, the

Washo could not adhere to a strict schedule of activities. Some informants remember the big times of the *gumsaba* lasting for as long as two weeks. The Washo felt that holding such gatherings were important in insuring an adequate harvest of piñon nuts, and many of the older Washo feel that abandoning the practice in modern times has caused poorer harvests.

Girl's Dance

Another important ceremony of Washo life was the "girl's dance" or puberty ceremony. This was intimately related to women's role as a gatherer. The ceremony, which is practiced in one form or another by Indians throughout the west and southwest, took place at the time of a girl's first menses. During this period a girl was urged to be active and not to be lazy. She was expected to move swiftly, running whenever possible, on her daily rounds of gathering. Whatever she gathered was made available to anyone who wanted it and of course was forbidden to her. Nor could she eat meat or salt, scratch herself, or comb her hair. In most cases she was expected to fast entirely during a four-day period, taking only cold water. At the end of the four days the girl's family would light a signal fire on a prominent peak as an invitation to all who saw it. When the neighboring families had assembled, a dance was held all during one night. During the dance the girl, often with a companion about her own age, carried a long straight wand of elderberry that was colored red with a special earth which had been collected and made into paint. Sometime during the night the girl, with a male companion, ran to the top of a nearby hill and lit several fires and then raced down to rejoin the crowd. At dawn a male relative would seize the elderberry wand and run away into the hills there to hide the wand in an upright position. It was believed that as long as the wand remained upright the girl would be straight and strong. If she had behaved properly during the dance and the four days preceding it, she would be hard working, energetic, self-effacing, able to withstand hunger, generous, and able to endure discomfort all of her life. As a final act of ceremony, the girl was taken to a nearby stream, lake or spring. There she was dusted with ashes while her sponsors prayed that she would be healthy, strong, generous, and hard working. They emphasized that this was done early in the morning so that she would always be an early riser and not be lazy. The ashes were washed from her body with water carried in a basket woven for the occasion. The basket was then thrown into the assembled crowd as a prize. The girl was daubed with red paint on her chest and face. The girl was now a woman and her family distributed gifts of food and shell beads to the assembled guests as something of a payment for being witness to this important change in their daughter's social status. The view that at the time of her first menses a girl was malleable and that her entire life would be shaped by the way she behaved at this time was widespread. The goal which the ceremony tried to achieve was to develop a woman devoted to the business of collecting food energetically throughout her life.

The Technology of the Piñon

Unlike other gathering activities, the piñon harvest could provide more food if a certain degree of cooperation existed. Two or three persons working together could gather many more nuts than a single person and thus a family would divide itself into two or three such groups. The basic tool of the piñon gatherer was a long pole with a smaller and, sometimes, curved stick attached. This could be used to knock piñon cones from the very topmost limbs of the pine tree. This method was not dissimilar from that used by "almond knockers" today. The knockers' companions gathered the fallen cones in baskets. Cones which had fallen naturally were gathered. A man and his wife working all day could collect the equivalent of one and one half or two gunny sacks of pine nuts. The gunny-sack measure is, of course, a result of white contact.

The nuts had to be removed from the cone and prepared by various cooking methods to prevent their spoilage. During a month of intense activity the Washo collected and prepared literally tons of piñon nuts to be stored against the winter. With the end of the harvest the Washo once again dispersed, moving toward the camps they would occupy during the winter. From the spring to the fall the Washo had moved from the west to the east of their heartland. Expeditions outside this area had taken them into the mountains and well into the peripheral areas of Washo country, but fishing on the west and gathering piñon nuts on the east marked the shift from one side of the heartland to the other. The trek to the winter camps was slow. The large supply of pine nuts was difficult to move. Without horses and wagons, the supply was moved on human backs. Often a move of only a few miles required several days. The old people and children watched the nut supply while the able-bodied members of the family moved back and forth. Basket loads of nuts were carried by a trump line across the chest by the women and with head bands by men, a device which kept their hands free for weapons. A few families might remain in the pine nut hills, but there were only a few springs there and the area was subject to heavy snow fall. Most families lived along the eastern edge of the Sierra on high ground to avoid floods and yet near firewood and water. Baskets of nuts were stored in specially prepared holes or in caves, and the families began to settle in for the winter. During the late summer women had collected the twigs of the willow to be used to weave into the baskets which served so many purposes in Washo life. The winter would be a time for basket weaving for the women and the chipping of arrowheads and the manufacturing of hunting weapons by the men. Baskets ranged from large loosely woven carrying baskets to small woven jugs which could hold water. Cooking was done in baskets, so tightly woven that they would hold water brought to a boil by dropping in heated stones. Other baskets were used to winnow the chaff from seeds, and babies were carried on their mothers' backs in basketry cradles. With the coming of winter, the gathering year was all but finished. If the gathering had been good during the summer, there would be supplies enough to last until spring. If not, starvation would haunt the Washo. The taking of ice-trapped fish might help fill out an empty winter larder, but for the most part hunting offered the only source of food in the winter.

The Hunting Year

We have seen that hunting began as soon as animals appeared in the spring. Game was taken whenever and wherever it was encountered throughout the year, but in the main, hunting occupied a brief period beginning in the late summer and lasting until the first snows of the winter. Hunting was exclusively a man's activity and one for which boys began training in their earliest childhood. Until a man was too old to endure the hardships of hunting trips he sought game constantly. Even in his old age he would devote his efforts to the taking of small game that a younger, more able-bodied man would scorn. Often these small game expeditions to trap and shoot chipmunks and squirrels were made up of old men and young boys. The old men thus passed on to children their lifetime of experience in the ways of animals and the lore of the hunt. Unlike plants which, despite their diversity of species, required a generally similar technique for collection, each type of animal demanded special skills if it was to be taken.

The basic Washo hunting weapon was a short bow backed with animal sinew to increase its power. Arrows were tipped with flint or obsidian heads attached to a light shaft which was inserted into the larger arrowshaft. Although popular thought sees the primitive hunter as an expert archer, he was probably far less accurate than a modern bowman shooting for sport. The Washo hunter was successful not because of uncanny accuracy but because of his stalking ability. The purpose of the hunt was to get close enough to the game so that a miss was virtually impossible. To accomplish this required years of training. A knowledge of wind and scent and how these combined to warn the quarry was essential as was muscle control to allow a hunter to move without attracting attention. Above all, a complete understanding of the habits of animals was essential to a successful stalk. Even for the experienced hunter possessed of all these skills, chance played an important part in any hunt. This uncertainty of outcome appears to be the basis of the superstructure of ritual and magic which surrounded Washo hunting life. If plant species matured, there was no doubt that the seeds or roots could be gathered. If the fish appeared at the right time, the mass fishing party or fish trap was certain to yield results. The hunter, however, never knew whether his efforts would produce game or not and so turned to the supernatural for assistance. In addition to physical and weapon-using skills and a knowledge of animal lore, a hunter had to learn the ritual and magic which were part of hunting. It was a long apprenticeship and a demanding one that was not complete until a youth was a young man. Because each species of animal required different skills and knowledge and different social responses, we will examine the hunting year in terms of the major species taken.

Rabbit

Spread throughout the lowlands of the Washo country and extending into the foothills, the western jack rabbit was the most commonly hunted animal. In rabbit hunting, cooperation produced greater results than solitary hunting and we find one of the relatively rare occasions for large-scale cooperative activities among the Washo.

In the fall, just after the pine nut harvest, the jack rabbit was common on the flatlands just to the east of the Sierra Nevada. A number of people walking in a line across the flats could scare up and drive before them hundreds of rabbits, still fat from their summer feeding. A man who was a good shot with a bow could kill a great many rabbits simply by joining such a drive. But this was not the most productive method of taking rabbits. The rabbits, slowly contained by a curving line of people, could be driven very easily into a long net and killed there with ease. Almost every Washo family owned such a net, several yards long, made of sage fibers. When supported on sticks, the nets were perhaps three feet high. If several families combined their nets, a barrier over a hundred yards long could be put up. With part of the group waiting behind the nets and the rest driving toward the barrier, a mornings' hunt could collect hundreds of jack rabbits weighing several pounds apiece. Hunts like this were staged throughout the Washo country wherever the rabbit population was high. Camps resembling small villages would spring up and each day the nets would be set up and a drive conducted across a different area until the rabbit population had been killed or driven out. During these times, just before the onset of winter, the Washo gorged themselves on fresh broiled rabbit. Hundreds more were skinned and cleaned and hung on racks to dry. In the dry air of the high steppes the rabbit carcasses dried into an unappetizing appearing, almost completely dehydrated, mummy. During the winter these dried rabbits would be pounded into powder and added to soups or to pine nut and grass seed mushes. In extremely good years many more rabbits would be killed than could be consumed. Their skins were stripped off and the carcasses left. The skins provided the material for the most important and in many cases the only clothing of the Washo, the rabbit-skin blanket. The fresh skins were cut into strips and these woven on a frame into a blanket which served as both cloak and bedding. The soft rabbit fur made a warm covering which wore out quickly, requiring frequent replenishment.

Deer

The fall was not the only time for rabbit hunting. The large wily animals were stalked by hunters through the spring and summer. Washo hunting seasons were often determined by the condition of the animals, so that fewer animals were taken in the spring when they were thin than in the late summer when they were fat and toothsome. As important as the rabbit was to Washo subsistence, the hunting year, that is the portion of the year in which hunting rather than fishing or gathering directed Washo movement and organization, began before rabbit hunting was at its peak.

The late summer was a time when gathering, save for the pine nuts, was falling off and when the men began to prepare for large-scale hunts for the winter meat. The most important animal after the rabbit was the deer. The hunting parties often traveled well beyond Washo country into the lands of the Maidu and the Miwok in California where the deer were more numerous. Usually, however, hunts were conducted in the territory along the eastern edge of the Sierra. In a time of need, deer would be taken whenever encountered, but the Washo preferred to hunt them from late August until early winter, after the fawns of the spring were large enough to fend for themselves and before the rutting season when the flesh of the buck deer was rank tasting. As the winter progressed, the deer became thinner and less desirable and were taken only if the Washo faced starvation.

A single species of deer, the California mule deer, inhabited the Washo country. The Washo language contains a single word, *memdewe,* for deer although the people differentiate between deer which drifted west in the fall and those which moved east into the Basin. Washo men hunted deer in a number of ways. Most frequently a man, alone or with one or two companions, went out from his camp in the morning to stalk deer during the daylight hours. One might simply move cautiously through the forest hoping to come upon a deer before it was aware of human presence. Far more frequent was a stalk using a disguise. Wearing a stuffed deer head with the skin attached and draped over his shoulders, the hunter would locate a group of grazing deer and then begin to close in on his quarry. Remaining always to windward so that his odor would not reveal the deception, the hunter would approach the herd, expertly imitating the actions of a buck approaching a strange group of his fellows. An experienced hunter could imitate a deer so well that the herd would return to browsing after his presence was noted. In this manner the hunter could come to within a few feet of his quarry before throwing off his disguise, and drawing his arrow to the head and loosing it. At these close ranges he seldom missed. The ideal target spot was the area just behind the shoulder. An arrow point in this vital area would penetrate the lungs, and the convulsive movement of the shoulder blade, as the animal plunged away, usually broke off the shaft leaving the head and foreshaft in the deer's body. An arrow lacks the shocking power of a bullet and no matter how well placed seldom kills outright. A grievously wounded deer when pursued can run for many miles and often evade the hunter. The Washo hunter avoided this possibility through an exercise of patience. If his arrow struck home, he immediately sat down to wait. If the arrowshaft had been broken off he examined it for blood stains. If he found blood, he mixed it with saliva, started a fire and heated a stone and placed the mixture on the stone. The liquid boiled away. When this happened, the hunter extinguished his fire and began to track his quarry. A wounded deer that is not pursued will usually stop after running a short distance, loss of blood and shock and stiffening muscles often force him to lie down. A hunter who has been patient will find the deer a short distance away, dead or dying, usually exuding a bloody froth from his nose and mouth. The Washo argued that the ritual of the hot stone was a magic act which actually killed the deer. A more objective observer might argue that it simply gave the hunter something to do while he waited for his arrow to take effect.

Stalking with a disguise was the business of an expert. Any movement which might cause suspicion in the herd he was stalking, a misstep or abrupt movement caused by cramped muscles, or impatience could send the deer flying. Moreover, the disguise itself was a matter of concern. As we will see later, the Washo considered the remains, particularly the bones, of animals killed for food as sacred and dangerous if not handled with respect and consideration. Thus the disguise consisting of skull and antlers was not something to be handled casually. In fact, many hunters feared using a disguise made of real antlers and substituted branches of the manzanita bush. There also was an element of physical danger, particularly as the hunting season moved into the fall. A rutting buck deer is prepared to fight all comers and an expert imitation might invite a charge. A full-grown buck mule deer may weigh 200 pounds and his antlers and sharp hooves are exceedingly dangerous weapons, more so to a man encumbered by a deer head and skin. Having once been attacked by a young mule deer buck weighing far less than the writer, he agrees with his Washo informants that the possibility of attack was not one to be taken lightly. The less expert hunter had a number of alternative methods for taking the deer. The most common was to build a blind of brush near a spring or salt lick and lay in wait for his quarry. This was a good method except that it limited the time when hunting might be successful. Unless a hunter was in position before the deer came to the lick or spring, his wait would be in vain. The stalker, on the other hand, could search through an area and find the deer, rather than waiting for them. Hunting expeditions such as this supplied fresh meat for the immediate family of the hunters with each member of the small party getting his share. However, as the year progressed into the fall before the mountains were filled with snow and the passes closed, deer hunting became the major activity of all Washo men. In this period, the purpose was to accumulate dried deer meat for winter food. To this end, larger hunting parties set out, leaving their families, often going into California to hunt intensively. Usually a hunting party was composed of six to eight men. An older man usually accompanied the party to tend the camp and cook. Perhaps a boy or two would go along to learn the business of hunting. Once encamped in a good hunting area, the party might split up each morning with each man setting out on a stalk of his own. If there were many deer in the area, a drive might be organized. One or two of the best shots would be stationed along a deer trail while the rest of the party spread out below them and began to walk toward the bowmen, making enough noise to disturb the deer and cause them to move away from the drivers. There was no attempt to stampede the deer. It was more productive to disturb them only enough to force them to move past the ambush. In the course of a day several such drives could produce a number of deer. As the daily kill was gathered, the animals were skinned and butchered and the meat cut into strips. The meat was hung on drying racks to dry. Only the neck was dried intact and brought home with the bone left in. This was considered especially good feed for children and old people and was never eaten by the hunters. The rest of the skeleton, save perhaps the head and antlers, was taken with great care and submerged in a stream so that scavengers would not disturb it. The Washo believed, as did most American Indians, that game animals voluntarily allowed themselves to be killed for the benefit of man. If man did not appreciate this sacrifice and treated the remains of his benefactors callously, the animals would refuse to be killed.

If the hunting was good, a party would remain in the forest for two weeks, or even a month, hunting until they had collected all the meat they could carry. With the meat boned and dried, a single man could carry the meat of several deer quite easily. Eighty to one hundred pounds was not considered too heavy for an able-bodied Washo man. Thus a hunting party of eight could, if its luck was good, bring home between 800 and a 1000 pounds of dried deer meat and hides. Occasionally, larger groups of Washo collected for deer hunting. In the early fall when the foliage in the foothills was dry, a large area might be surrounded and set on fire to drive the deer into the open to be shot. The Washo also constructed a simple noose trap, suspended along a deer trail which could catch and choke a deer, although this method appears to have been rare.

Two other large game animals played a role, although not so important as that of the deer, in supplying meat for the Washo cooking baskets. To the north and south and farther to the east, pronghorned antelope appeared in great numbers but the Washo territory lay between the northern and southern ranges and in this area the pronghorn was not too plentiful. Nonetheless, when it could be taken it was, and the method is one of the most interesting links between the culture of the Washo and that of their neighbors in the Basin to the east.

Antelope

The antelope is an extremely fleet and sharp-eyed creature. Living on the flat steppes as it does, it is able to see danger at a great distance and flee from it. However, the antelope has two weaknesses which enabled the American Indian to develop successful techniques for hunting it. It is a herd animal, preferring to remain with its fellows even in the face of danger, and it is incurably curious. Early white hunters report that they were often able to lure antelope into gun range by simply waving a white cloth on a stick. Eventually, curiosity overcame caution and the pronghorns would come to investigate the strange sight. For the Indian without firearms the antelope had to be brought into even closer range than was necessary for the hunter armed with a rifle. An occasional skillful hunter could stalk an individual antelope and kill it with a bow. Or a group of hunters could occasionally form a drive similar to that employed in deer hunting. But the most common and most productive method was the surrounding or corralling method. When the presence of a herd of antelope was known, the people who had discovered it would send out the word to their neighbors to form a communal hunt. The first step in such an undertaking was to build a corral of brush or rope made of sagebrush bark. Occasionally brush would be piled at intervals to form a circle, the spaces to be filled by people at the time of the hunt. Frequently, wings would be built extending out from the opening of the corral. Once the corral had been finished, young men were sent to place themselves on the side of the herd away from the corral and slowly drive the antelope toward the trap. Moving slowly and keeping concealed in order not to stampede the herd, the drivers crept close, then one at a time, suddenly stood up and then just as suddenly hid themselves. These strange appearances made the herd nervous and generally forced it to move slowly toward the corral. As the herd approached closer, more and more people joined in the drive, appearing in every quarter save the direction of the trap. Soon the pressure of the human presence became more and more intense and active. Finally, at the entrance to the corral, the erstwhile quiet and cautious drive became noisy. The antelope were stampeded into the trap and the opening closed. Once the animals were contained there was usually ritual dancing and singing, often lasting all night. The trap and the sounds of the people surrounding them panicked the herd and drove the antelope around and around the corral until by dawn of the next morning they were exhausted. A specially selected archer killed the first antelope before the general slaughtering began. A herd of antelope could supply food for a relatively large number of people for several days, perhaps a week. The people would then disperse to continue their regular hunting and gathering rounds. One such hunt usually exhausted the antelope population in an area and would not be repeated there for several years.

Throughout most of the Great Basin the antelope hunt was a singularly important activity inasmuch as it brought together, for a short time at least, a large number of people cooperating and operating under a form of political authority absent in all other areas of their lives. Almost predictably, the entire process of the antelope drive was surrounded by an aura of sacredness and ritual. The discovery of a herd was always announced by a man with special power, an antelope shaman, who was believed to have the ability to locate a herd of antelope and charm them into the corral through the use of special magic. Most frequently, the shaman discovered the presence of the antelope in a dream and upon awakening made his announcement and sent messengers to inform the neighboring people. While the preparations were underway, he prayed and sang, weaving a spell of magic to charm the antelope to their deaths. The details of the hunt and its accompanying ritual varied greatly throughout the Basin, but it always had its supernatural element and the antelope shaman with his special power. Some groups believed that antelope power was so great that when used it invariably killed one of the members of the hunting group. This loss was considered as part of the cost of social survival for the group. For the few days of the hunt the shaman assumed political power inasmuch as he could direct the activities of the group. This phenomenon of the general pattern varying in detail from place to place has been called a "culture trait complex" and has been reported throughout the world in many areas of human activity. The Washo, living in the extreme west of the Great Basin and speaking a different language, displayed this "trait complex" in its least complicated form. There were, for instance, among the Washo no special antelope shaman. Any "dreamer," a person gifted with the power to receive prophetic dreams, might discover the presence of a herd. He would then become the leader of the drive. The use of magic by the leader was absent. What magic or ritual there was was conducted by the entire population engaged in the hunt. The entire hunting group observed a taboo against sexual intercourse during the hunting, and menstruating women could not take part in the hunt. The Washo considered the belief that a person would die as a result of an antelope hunt as a somewhat silly superstition. The antelope hunt as carried out by the Washo is an excellent example of another cultural phenomenon known as diffusion or borrowing of traits of behavior from neighboring people. Inasmuch as all such complexes are made up of a number of discrete traits, not all of which are necessary to the basic purpose of the complex, they may diffuse piecemeal from culture to culture. The Washo, alert to any environmental opportunity, would naturally want to hunt the antelope whenever possible. It is clear that they looked to the other cultures of the Basin for an example of how the antelope could be best taken. Thus we see the drive into a trap, but not the building of a corral. The Washo borrowed the practical aspects of the antelope hunt but rejected the ritual superstructure which had meaning to the neighboring Paiute and Shoshone. The Washo followed their own traditional patterns as to dreaming power and group magic and temporary leaders. We can also see that the Washo, who hunted antelope rather infrequently, were not as knowledgeable about this species as they were about the deer. Individual Washo hunters seldom, if ever, attempted to stalk antelope, apparently lacking the knowledge and skill to undertake this difficult job, although Paiute and Shoshone hunters frequently used this method.

Sheep and Bear

One other species of large game played a role in the pattern of Washo subsistence, although it was even less important than the antelope. In the Sierra to the west and in the dry desert mountains to the east there were populations of mountain sheep, a subspecies of the Rocky Mountain bighorn and a variety of desert bighorn. The Washo made no distinction between what we see as two different types of animals. Both were called *ogul*. The wild sheep was even more difficult to hunt than the antelope, living in the remote and rugged wildness of the high country, often above timberline. Keen eyed and agile, they were difficult to stalk. Nonetheless, occasional parties of expert hunters went into the mountains in the early fall when the first snows had driven the animals down from their summer haunts among the peaks. There, a careful hunter might stalk and surprise a sheep, which often weighed more than a man. The most frequent means of taking the mountain sheep was by applying a knowledge of animal habits. The sound of two rams fighting, their great curving horns smashing together in a headlong charge often attracted other rams and curious ewes. Indians throughout the sheep country took advantage of this and learned to imitate the sounds of fighting by striking sticks together. This usually drew the quarry close enough so that a hunter could shoot them from ambush.

The black bear was common in the Washo country and at least a few grizzlies are known to have inhabited the area, but the bear played a very minor role in Washo subsistence. In cases of extreme emergency, bear meat might be eaten but in general bear hunting was more of a ritual than an economic or subsistence activity. Like most primitive people living in the northern hemisphere, the Washo considered the bear a very special, if not sacred, animal possessed of enormous supernatural power. To kill a bear assured a man's reputation as a hero and possessor of great power. A bear hunt was not, properly speaking, a hunt at all. A number of men would band together and locate the winter lair of a hibernating bear. One of their number would enter the lair armed with a torch and an arrow or knife to prod the beast awake and then flee outside. As the bear, still groggy from months of sleep and blinded by the light, stepped out of his lair, the waiting companions fired arrows into the animal, aiming for the mouth in particular. The hide, a symbol of bravery and power, was taken by the man whose arrow first hit the animal and the meat might be eaten by the members of the party but it was not divided among the various families. A Washo legend tells of a time when a band of Paiutes bent on marauding were so cowed by seeing the Washo kill a bear that they decamped and fled as if they had been beaten in battle.

Birds

In addition to the mammals hunted regularly, many species of birds and wild fowl nested in the Washo country. The sinks and swamps in the eastern valleys provided nesting for a dozen or more species of water fowl and the sage flats and foothills were the home of quail, sage hens, prairie chickens, and doves. When great numbers of birds were present in the lowland lakes, many tribes, including the Washo, might camp on the shores and stage drives. Using a boat made of tule, the birds could be herded together and taken in large numbers. When the fowl were fat and found it difficult to fly, they could be taken by hand. In shallow bodies of water a rabbit net might be used and birds driven into it by hunters wading in the water. Small arrowheads were made for bird hunting and used by hunters stalking along the shores of a lake or sink. When the young were partially grown but still unable to fly, they were gathered up by parties of hunters, who always left enough to insure a crop in the following year. While the various Paiute bands might have a special chief to direct the waterfowl drive as they did for an antelope hunt, the Washo simply gathered together and cooperated in such an endeavor without formal leadership. Land birds were taken with bow and arrow, an easy task when pursuing large flocks of relatively large birds like the sage hen and prairie chicken. Some hunters made a special arrowhead with a guard of four crossed sticks to increase the chances of hitting a bird in flight. Snares and traps might also be used to take birds. The most productive period for bird hunting was once again in late summer and fall, although some species of water fowl nested throughout the winter in the Washo country and served as a source of food during periods of starvation. The limitation on the utility of fowl as food was technical. There is no evidence that any attempt was made to preserve birds by drying so that the take had to be consumed soon after the hunt to avoid spoilage. Fresh birds swelled the diet and reduced the pressure on stored food such as pine nut flour and dried deer meat. Birds appeared to be considered what in modern military language we would call a "target of opportunity." That is, very little general planning went into bird hunting. If they were present, they were taken, but seldom do Washo informants speak of shifting camp or making special long trips to hunt either waterfowl or upland game birds.

Other Animals

In times of starvation the Washo would eat any animal which could be taken, but, in general, they seemed to have weighed very carefully the effort against the return. Many fur-bearing animals were taken if they were encountered, their pelts being useful for clothing, blankets, or arrow quivers. Only the wild cat, muskrat, fox, and badger among the fur bearers are reported to have been eaten at all regularly. The porcupine, slow footed and slow witted and easily killed by even a child with a stick, was also a regular source of food. The woodchuck, common in the mountain country, was also a favorite target for hunters. There were many varieties of squirrels throughout the Washo territory and they were regularly taken. Adult hunters seldom set out specifically to hunt squirrel, but older men past their prime and young boys learning their trade hunted squirrel with both bow and traps.

The gopher and the ground squirrel were considered less than game and were frequently taken by women who smoked them out of their holes or flooded them out by diverting nearby streams. A split stick which would entangle in the hair of a rodent was poked into a hole and twisted until the gopher or squirrel was entrapped and could be pulled out. A number of lesser rodents, field mice and even moles, were occasionally eaten if they could be taken in large enough number to justify the effort. The unique kangaroo rat found in the flatlands of the valleys was also taken and eaten.

In general, once the fishing season was over, the taking of birds and mammals was a continuous activity, contributing substantially to the daily food supply. Hunting with the bow was an exclusive male function which often took men away from their families. Small animals and animals which could be taken in large number were the quarry of both men and women, often working together. In the last months of the summer and in the fall, hunting became a major activity as part of the preparations for winter. In the case of the rabbit and, less commonly, the antelope, the occurrence of these animals led to a movement of campsites.

Insects and Reptiles

The people of the Great Basin were always alert to any opportunity to gather food in quantity and so the insect life of the area was not overlooked. Periodically the locusts swarmed and migrated, covering an area with what was almost a blanket of voracious insect life. The Washo always rallied to gather as many of them as possible. Sometimes the insects would be gathered in baskets and roasted in the coals of a camp fire. At other times brush and grass was set on fire and the insects driven by the flames into a ditch where they could be gathered more easily. Dried and ground, they produced a nutritious and long lasting flour to be mixed with other foods.

At certain times of the year the common grasshopper appeared in great numbers. If a gatherer began early in the morning before the hoppers became active in the growing warmth of the day, he could pick them from the grass and bushes with ease. These were usually roasted in pits. The grasshopper could also be dried and ground into flour to be stored against the winter.

Bees' nests provided not only honey, which was consumed on the spot, but the "eggs," or larvae of the bee, were cooked and eaten. Although ants and ant eggs were eaten by all the neighboring people, the Washo stubbornly insist that they never used the ant as food. They did, however, eat caterpillars whenever they appeared in sufficient numbers to justify gathering them.

Long trips were often made south to Mono Lake, an awesome body of water so filled with minerals that no fish lived there. However, a small grub thrived in this water and often washed on the shore in great number. This grub, known as *matsibabesha* by the Washo, was gathered as food and as a powerful medicine or magic substance useful in bringing fishing luck.

Most reptiles and amphibians were avoided as food, but certain large lizards were considered to be worth taking and were killed and cooked whenever encountered.

The Culture of Hunting

Hunting and the more energetic forms of fishing were the domain of the Washo male and his training began in his early childhood. The ritual connected with hunting served to emphasize the importance of hunting and symbolize the division of labor between the sexes. All hunting and fishing equipment used by men was taboo to women, particularly menstruating women. If a woman handled a man's bow or his arrows or touched his fish harpoon, it was felt necessary to give the piece of equipment a ritual bath and say a number of prayers to restore its usefulness. To ignore this would certainly bring bad luck. Before a man set out to hunt, he bathed and sang prayerful songs. Usually he rubbed himself with the leaves of a certain plant to bring hunting luck. This may have helped obscure the human odor and made stalking easier.

As a boy grew into manhood, his hunting adventures became more and more demanding. Gradually he graduated from mice or wood rats to squirrels and then to woodchuck and game birds and the stalking of rabbits. During all this period he was never allowed to eat any animal he killed. Usually he gave this game away to neighbors or relatives, displaying at once the Washo virtue of generosity and learning the important lesson of mutual dependance and, incidentally, building up a number of small debts which he might some day call in if he needed food or assistance. Finally, as he became expert, a lad would attempt to kill a full-grown buck deer. If he was successful, the kill was of course, taboo to him but the event marked his transition to full manhood. He would be ritually bathed by his father or grandfather, who were also forbidden to eat the meat. The antlers of the deer would be set on their points and the naked boy would attempt to crawl through them. If he had killed a buck large enough to permit this, he was considered to have entered the status of adult hunter and incidentally to be a candidate for marriage.

So uncertain was the business of hunting that Washo men continually sought or at least hoped for assistance from the supernatural. Successful hunters were always considered to have special powers which allowed them to charm their quarry and make hunting easier. The Washo believed the neighboring California tribes had special medicine which put whole herds of deer to sleep. A hunter with medicine kept it secret and did not boast about it or pass the secret on to others. Hunting virtually dominated the Washo man's image of himself. Even today to suggest that a man had no taste for hunting and preferred to remain in camp with the women is an oblique way of attacking his entire character. The ritual of hunting, preserving the usefulness of his weapons, the respect shown to the hunted animal all combined in a pattern of behavior which influenced most of the day-to-day routine of a Washo man. We have seen earlier that the coming of age ceremonies of a young woman emphasized the womanly virtues of industry, generosity, and steady application to the business of collecting plant food. For the boy, the occasion was related to hunting which was the main occupation of men.

Trade

Hunting and gathering supplied virtually all the necessities of Washo life: food, what little clothing was worn, housing, and the tools and weapons needed to hunt and gather and prepare food. However, the Washo were not entirely self-contained. Areas outside the Washo country offered desirable goods which the Washo got through trade or by means of long gathering ventures far outside their home territory. The Washo country was inhabited by many more deer than was the region to the east, while further out in the Basin the antelope population was higher. Although they often fought each other, the Washo engaged in a lively trade with the Paiute, exchanging deer hides for those of the antelope. Occasionally, a buffalo hide obtained by the Paiute from peoples farther east would come into Washo hands to be traded west to California Indians. The need for salt and for mineral earths with which to make paints was often the excuse for the forming of expeditions to foreign territory to collect these materials. Obsidian for arrow points was sometimes gathered in this manner or obtained through trade.

The Washo, living between the rich country of California and the relatively impoverished Basin served as trade agents for many desirable goods from the west. Inasmuch as they had little that the California tribes could not obtain for themselves, the Washo frequently had to undertake long journeys to obtain trade articles. Tribal tradition recalls long trips during the summer which took families to the shores of the Pacific to gather shell fish. The mollusks were eaten on the spot but great packs of shells were carried back over the Sierra to be made into jewelry and ritual objects and to be traded to the people to the east. Bands of young men are said to have traveled as far south as San Diego to obtain particularly fine obsidian knives from the tribes in that region. The Yosemite Valley was well known to the Washo who viewed the area from the surrounding mountains. They were afraid to enter the valley because of a belief that the Indians who lived there were sorcerers. This wide network of travel made the Washo aware of the customs of many people and, as we shall see, served to spread some of these customs.

Summary

In this section we have examined Washo life in terms of the subsistence activities which supported the tribe. We see that hunting, gathering, and fishing each played an important role in supporting the Washo and in determining their annual movements. We have seen too that no single resource could be counted on to provide food and other necessities throughout the entire year. To take advantage of the varied opportunities of their homeland, the Washo developed an opportunistic culture able to change plans on a moment's notice and seize the main chance as it presented itself. Seldom actually starving, but equally seldom able to relax in the search for food, the Washo survived because of their ability to adjust to conditions. Few rules of Washo life were so rigid as to resist the demands of subsistence. Even the taboo of women hunting was broken by widows forced to fend for themselves and their families. Ceremonies were lengthened and shortened as resources permitted, campgrounds shifted around as food supplies appeared and disappeared.

With such a simple technology to use in exploitation, the Washo was unable to depend on tools and machines or manufactured goods to protect him from the vagaries of his environment. In place of technology, the Washo used his own social organization. Washo society can be viewed as a mechanism which exploited the environment while satisfying the basic social needs of all human beings. In the next section we will examine the various aspects of Washo social structure as a series of task forces, each designed to provide for human needs.

5

Society and Culture

EVERY SOCIETY must function in such a way that its members are able to survive physically. If the society and its culture are to survive, social organization must provide a framework in which children can be conceived, born, and raised according to the traditions of their parents. Various societies meet these challenges in different ways, organizing themselves differently to meet different environmental and technical needs. The Washo environment was such that while it would provide a living for the energetic and alert, it provided very little margin for the elaboration of social institutions. Like many societies with a simple technology, the various social units had to perform multiple functions. For the Washo, social units had to be able to move quickly to take advantage of environmental opportunities and not exhaust the resources too quickly. The need for large-scale cooperation was minimal but not entirely absent. Hostile neighbors both to the east and west required that the Washo be able to muster enough fighting men to repel invaders. Social needs such as the change in status of a girl to that of young woman required the presence of as many people as possible. A number of subsistence activities, as we have seen, were more productive if a number of people could cooperate. The seemingly universal need of men to find identity in a group worked to encourage large gatherings of people whenever possible. However, the Washo could not live together for very long periods of time lest the food supply in any single area give out. Thus, we can examine the Washo social organization in terms of a series of groups of expanding size based on a single unit, the family.

The Family

The term family is best used to describe that social unit which has the responsibility of producing and training children, although even in everyday English the word has other connotations. Among the Washo the family unit

38

bore a heavy burden of responsibility besides caring for children. It was the basic economic unit, moving in search of food, without consideration for any other such group. Occasionally hunting trips might break up even this small unit, but in general it remained together, traveling, collecting food, and interacting with other families when the demands of nature or society called for or made cooperation possible. There are few households recorded with less than five members and even fewer with as many as a dozen. The relationships of the members were extremely varied and there seems to have been no set rule about who might join together to make a family.

In the eyes of the Washo, what we would call a family was identified with a single dwelling place, the winter house, or *galesdangl*. This was a crude home made of tree limbs leaning together to form a peak with a door in one end. Sometimes the *galesdangl* was covered with earth. In the valleys it might be made of brush or thatched with tule. This structure was used in the winter and unless a person died in the house, it was reused by the same people every winter. In the event of death, the house was torn or burned down and the spot abandoned in favor of a new winter location. The "family" they might be better referred to as the houshold, because the Washo tended to identify the group with the house. Usually, the basis of a *galesdangl* was a man and his wife and their children. A widow or widower, particularly if there were grown sons, might be the head of the household. In this case, the sons' wives might also join the group during the early part of their marriage or until the parent died. On other occasions brothers and sisters and their spouses occupied a single house and traveled together. Sometimes completely unrelated persons or "friends" joined a household. The Washo were occasionally polygynous, particularly if a first wife was barren. If a man married more than one woman, his wives might live in separate *galesdangl* quite close together or they might live in a single house. One man who married three sisters built two structures, one housing two wives and their children and the second serving as the home for the third wife and her children. This second home was soon filled by an unrelated man and later his wife and their children.

In many societies there are rather strict rules concerning where a newly married couple may live. In general, societies can be divided into matrilocal, those which require residence with the wife's parents; patrilocal, those requiring residence with the family of the husband; and neolocal, those requiring a newly married couple to set up housekeeping on their own. All three types of postmarital residence are reported in about equal number by the Washo. It is clear that the subsistence pattern of the Washo would not permit fixed adherence to any rule of residence. If one or another set of in-laws already had a large family, the addition of a son or daughter in-law might impose an insupportable burden on the ability of the entire group to survive. If, on the other hand, one of the parental families was shorthanded, the addition of an able-bodied hunter or an energetic gatherer might be welcomed.

Courtship, the first step in establishing another household, was relatively simple. Marriages were a matter of concern for the entire family. Occasions such as the girl's dance, or the *gumsaba,* were of course times for getting acquainted between eligible young men and women. If a son or daughter displayed interest in a particular person, his or her family would consider the person's working ability before encouraging the match. If both families agreed, there was often a prolonged exchange of small gifts before the mating became "official." Older Washo speak of a native ceremony of placing a blanket over the shoulders of a couple and having a respected elder lecture them on the responsibilities of marriage and parenthood.

A young man and wife constituted a partnership of skills: he a hunter and fisherman with many years of training; she a gatherer, cook, and basket weaver. By following their sexually determined activities, such a pair could easily provide for themselves. When a woman became pregnant and had a child, her ability to work was reduced until the child was weaned. Therefore, a household could easily use an older woman or a younger unmarried woman to assist with the gathering and home-making tasks. A successful hunter could provide for such a household with little trouble. Frequently the additional member of a household would be an aged parent no longer in his or her prime but able to contribute to the food supply by gathering or hunting small game. These oldsters were particularly helpful in caring for and instructing the children as they were weaned and forced to depend less and less on their mother. Anthropologists Stanley Freed and Ruth Freed have noted that even today an unusual warmth exists between relatives three generations apart, which seems to reflect this old relationship between the young and the old.

Not infrequently, a woman would urge that her husband seek another wife to assist her or to keep her company, or if she was barren, to provide children for the family to raise and care for. She often suggested a younger sister with whom she had been raised. The Washo felt this was a good solution inasmuch as women brought up together would be fond of each other and not fight. Moreover, a sister's children were closely related and could depend on loving care from their aunt should their mother die. Sometimes plural marriage was encouraged by a girl's parents. If a young man was particularly energetic in his hunting and fishing and had a reputation as a good provider, a girl's family would suggest that she attract his attention and become a second wife. A much rarer form of marriage, polyandry, in which a woman married more than one man was also practiced among the Washo. Such cases are infrequent and appear to have been temporary, that is, a woman married to one man also acted as wife to his younger brother. Her children were treated as offspring of the trio, but when the second brother married he left the children with his older brother and the woman. This arrangement seems to have developed as a result of the practice of the levirate. This is a widespread custom in which the widow of a man frequently marries one of his brothers. Inasmuch as a younger brother is a potential spouse and sexual partner, the exigencies of Washo life appear to have made it advantageous in some cases for the potential situation to become actualized until the younger brother found a wife of his own. It is possible that the marriage left the younger brother without a family unit and so he joined the new unit formed by the marriage of his brother. A woman with two adult men hunting for her was in a fortunate position and the extension of sexual privileges to the second brother may have symbolized her desire to maintain the situation. It is also probable that should her husband die she would have joined the household of the surviving brother as a second wife, thus transforming that which had begun as a relatively rare polyandrous marriage into the more common polygynous one. It was also a common practice for a man whose wife had died to marry one of her surviving sisters, a practice known as the sororate, which is also reflected in the frequency of polygynous marriages in which a man married two sisters.

As a family grew in size due to the birth of children, it might also grow through the addition of other relatives. Sisters or brothers left orphaned by the death of parents might join the household. Or, if the parental household was large, a younger sibling might find welcome in the household of his sister or brother where an extra hunter or gatherer would be useful. Widowed aunts or cousins might also join a household. The able were expected to do their share in the quest for food and the aged did what they could. Washo ethics demanded that the aged be cared for and supported by the group. Clearly, no household could successfully support too many ancients or too many small children.

It was the household group which moved in search of food, leaving the winter camp for Lake Tahoe and from there moving on the various rounds of the spring and summer and finally moving east to the pine nut hills. There the family would pick nuts from a plot marked off with stones. If a member of another group trespassed without permission, the owners of the plot could break his gathering pole and seize the nuts he had collected. A family inherited little else than the gathering plot inasmuch as a *galesdangl* was destroyed because of a death and all the dead person's personal property was destroyed or buried. Each spouse had the right to pick pine nuts on the plot used by his or her parents. A husband can gather on the wife's plot and she on his but with the death of a spouse, that right terminated. In addition to pine nut gathering rights, the family tended to have property rights in other areas. Fishing traps and platforms were generally considered the property of the family which built them and could be reclaimed from year to year and their use denied to others. The right to hunt eagles in a certain area was passed from father to son. The eagle was considered an exceedingly powerful bird, a messenger to the spirit world. His feathers were objects of great power and value and could be traded for almost anything an Indian found desirable. Taking eagles was a difficult and dangerous task requiring patience, courage, and skill. Young eaglets could be taken from the nest when discovered, risking, of course, the ire of the parents who might return during the robbery. The aeries were owned by an individual hunter who passed the right to take birds from that location on to his sons.

It is common today for Washo to claim leadership roles by referring to the fact that his father or some other paternal ancestor held such a position. He might even pick a maternal relative as a basis for his claim. This reflects a general tendency to bilateral descent and inheritance, but it is difficult to determine whether leadership roles were actually inherited in aboriginal times. There is some doubt that aboriginal "chiefs" or "captains" were much more than re-spected men whose advice had been found wise and was heeded by his friends, relatives, and neighbors.

Within the family the father appears to have had a great deal of authori-ty, particularly in dealing with his sons. He and his brothers most frequently taught a boy to hunt and told him tribal lore. A girl was the responsibility of the women of the household, who taught her the skills of gathering, cooking, and weaving, and sponsored her girl's dance. The family spent much of the year alone or in the company of a few other such groups. It was the core of Washo life. Training in the skills of adulthood and in Washo tradition and ethics were learned in the family. It was at one time a biological unit, conceiving, produc-ing, and nurturing children; an economic unit, gathering and hunting the food needed by its members; and an educational institution wherein were learned all the basic behavior patterns of Washo life. Inasmuch as there was little authority in Washo life, the family might also be considered a minimal political unit as well, allying to and cooperating with other such units but bound by no laws to follow any desires other than its own.

The family was the unit wherein, not surprisingly, we find most of the rituals of Washo life. This complex of rituals served to symbolize the limits of this family group and re-emphasize its unity and the importance of the mem-bers one to the other. Not until adolescence are outsiders really needed for the ceremonies of life.

Birth

In the popular mind, childbirth among primitive peoples is often viewed as a casual almost animal-like event. All of us have heard stories of how women disappear into the jungle and return with a child, ready to continue with their chores as if nothing had happened. Although this may be true in some parts of the world, it does not apply to the Washo or to any of their neighbors. The birth of a child was an event of enormous importance surrounded by a complex of ritual acts. Anthropologist Omer C. Stewart, who compiled trait lists for all the northern Paiute groups as well as the Washo, lists over two pages of taboos and ritual acts associated with birth. Of the over one hundred special birth cus-toms mentioned, the Washo are reported to have practiced over fifty. In short, in the matter of birth ceremonies the Washo were clearly part of a complex common to all the tribes of northern Nevada.

During her pregnancy a woman observed no particular rituals or taboos save that she was expected to work hard and remain active. The birth took place in a regular dwelling house, *galesdangl,* or *gadu,* and the mother was attended by older female relatives, or friends if no older relative was available. Delivery was achieved in a prone position. When the baby was born it was bathed, wrapped in some soft material, and placed on a winnowing basket. When the afterbirth appeared, it was wrapped in bark and buried. If a woman wished to have no more children, the pack was buried upside down. If at a later date she wished to have children, the spot where the afterbirth had been buried was turned over. A newly delivered woman was considered to be in extremely delicate condition and had to rest on a special bed until "her insides had healed." The special bed was a shallow pit filled with heated sand and covered with grass. Here the mother remained for an indefinite period, some informants insisting a month or six weeks, others stating that no specified time was required. During this post partum confinement, the mother was not allowed to eat meat or salt. Nor could she work or scratch herself with her fingers, being required instead to use a special scratching stick. Water was warmed before she was allowed to drink it and she was not permitted to bathe. When the father was notified of the birth, he went to the nearest stream and bathed. When he had finished, he left a deer skin or other valuable object on a bush near the edge of the water as a present for anyone who wished to take it. While his wife remained on her bed, the new father was required to remain extremely active, gathering fire wood and hunting every day. He was supposed to avoid gambling and smoking, and he could eat no meat, salt, or grease. At nights he remained awake as long as possible. His behavior was thought to insure that the child would be industrious and able to endure discomfort and hardship in its life. Sexual intercourse was forbidden to both parents and some informants say that this taboo was in effect for six months to a year.

When the infant's umbilical cord fell off, the mother announced it to the father who immediately went hunting and killed some animal which he brought home and distributed among the people of the household. On this day, anyone not related to the family could come and take whatever he wanted from among the father's possessions. It may be that this practice was thought to instill generosity in the infant or, perhaps, it created a debt which in future life the child could call in, making him not entirely dependant on his immediate family. The umbilical cord was tied to the right side of the baby's winnowing basket in the belief that this would make the baby right handed. About one month after the birth, a "baby feast," or *gumga.au*, was held by the family. The Washo word means literally hair cutting, and during the ceremony the mother bathed herself for the first time since the birth and had her own and her child's hair cut. The mother was assisted by another woman who dipped sagebrush in water and brushed it onto the mother and then ran her hands over the mother. The first haircut from the baby's head was wrapped in buckskin and attached to the hood of a basket cradle-board where the baby would rest from that time on. The winnowing basket which served as a bed for the infant was filled with various kinds of food and a few valuable items such as a bow, arrow, or eagle feather. The mother took some of the food, mixed it with sage leaves, chewed the mixture and then spat it out. After that the food and valuables were given away, the old being the chief beneficiaries, perhaps a ritual symbolism of the relation between the very young and the very old. After the ceremony, the taboos on meat, salt, grease, scratching, and, some say, sexual intercourse were removed and the parents could resume their normal lives.

Naming was not an important occasion among the Washo because an individual might have a great number of names in the course of his lifetime. A child was usually referred to by a baby name calling attention to some peculiarity of gait, appearance, behavior, or language. Later this name would be dropped in favor of an adult name reflecting some important event in his life or some idiosyncrasy of appearance or behavior. This name might change a number of times if events of hunting, war, or supernatural significance took place. When a person died his name was considered taboo and other persons with the same or similar names as the deceased usually dropped their names and chose another.

During childhood the loss of a milk tooth was an occasion of some minor ritual. The tooth was taken by an adult and thrown away. As he did this, the adult shouted to the small burrowing animals in the neighborhood, those with hard sharp teeth, that the milk tooth should be taken and exchanged for a strong tooth in the child's mouth.

The girl's dance was sponsored by her parents but required the presence of as many people as possible as participants. However, it was within the family group itself that a Washo child learned of a host of ritual activities and seemingly pointless acts which tied Washo society together and emphasized the Washo distinctness from all other people. Within the family one learned of the basic separation between men and women and of the important taboos associated with this. Girls learned of the need to protect the hunting weapons and fishing equipment of their men folk against defilement by menstruation. Boys learned to avoid this contaminating influence. Boys also began to learn hunting ritual and magic from their fathers while girls learned the role of women. Young girls and unmarried women were cautioned not to comb their hair at night lest they marry non-Washo strangers and become lost to their tribe. They learned that a woman in confinement would become wrinkled if she wiped perspiration from her face instead of dabbing it off. Taboos concerning dangerous foods were taught along with the skills needed to identify and gather desirable foods. Omens such as the hooting of an owl around camp, which presaged a death, were taught in the family circle. Girls were taught to avoid bats as creatures which would endanger their virtue. Boys were told of the power of various animals and how to overcome it. In short, the Washo family was a self-contained unit, composed of the right number of people to most efficiently exploit the environment and functioning to train children to become adult Washo with very little dependence on institutions outside its own limits. In reality, a Washo family was seldom totally alone. Winter camps were usually composed of from four to ten *galesdangle* within a short distance of each other and the various families tended to move together in an informal but recognized social unit called the "bunch." This unit seems to have been what we have come to call a band but we will retain the Washo-English term to distinguish it from the more rigidly defined group.

The Bunch

Despite the pressures of the past century, the dislocations and disorganization brought about by white intrusion, the Washo family remains a constant and with it much of the old ritual. The need for a social unit to produce, nurture, and train children is renewed each generation. The last "bunch" ceased to exist in Washo life sometime in the 1920s and with it much of the knowledge about its function. One is led to believe that as important as the unit was in aboriginal and early historical times, its existence was dependent on a set of environmental and social factors which are no longer present. The size and composition of the various "bunches" recorded by anthropologists over the past decades vary a great deal, and clearly the unit seemed to be in a constant state of formation, dissolution and re-formation in response to the environment and the accidents of the individual lives of its members. The winter camp or village of several households appears to be the basis of the bunch, although if several such villages were fairly close together and tended to move together they might be considered as part of a single bunch. Most frequently a bunch was identified with its leader and would be referred to as "so and so's bunch." The assumption of leadership of a bunch was an informal matter. A man with a reputation for wisdom, generosity, humility, and good humor would gradually assume the leadership role among his neighbors. His advice would be sought about hunting and gathering, and his directions, always given reluctantly and obliquely, would be followed in group activities such as a rabbit hunt or a dance. A man with special power was more likely to become a leader than was a man without power. A person noted for his power to dream the presence of rabbit or antelope or foretell the spawning run of fish was a useful man to have in one's group. In English these men were often called a "rabbit boss" or "antelope boss." They would notify their neighbors of the possibility or advisability of a hunt and then direct the group's activities. Although his powers were limited specifically to the single sphere, his importance to his neighbors tended to encourage their turning to him for counsel.

Usually men of the same "bunch" joined together to form hunting parties. The bunch might as a unit move to the west side of the Sierra to pick acorns or go to the ocean to gather shells for trading. In time of emergency the men of the bunch usually stood together in defense of attacks from raiders from the neighboring tribes. These groups might ally themselves with the men of other bunches to form large war parties or repel a large enemy party, although they appear to have been under no compulsion to do so. In general, we might say that the bunch consisted of a minimal number of families that could cooperate to do those things which an individual family could not do for itself— stage rabbit drives, form hunting parties, defend itself, and so on. The size of such a group might vary from year to year or even from week to week. Should a family decide to move to some area where they had heard that a good gathering crop was available, they were in no way compelled to remain with their erstwhile companions. Single families or groups of families might separate to hunt or gather in areas where the entire group could not find sustenance. Later they might rejoin the original group or, if they chose, ally themselves with some other bunch. Most often, the various families were related by blood or marriage, but there appears to have been no bar to unrelated families joining the group. In the course of events, as children grew to adulthood and married, they would become relatives.

We have seen that the Washo abandoned a house in which a person had died and moved away from the spot. Therefore, a family experiencing a death might of necessity have to seek a camp with another bunch for the winter. Young people might leave the bunch or join it as the situation dictated when they married. Personal animosities were often resolved by the removal of one of the parties to another area. Thus the bunch remained relatively the same size through the years, but its members, both families and individuals, changed frequently.

There was a tendency for the descendants of leaders to become leaders themselves, leading some to speak of inheritance. It is more probable that a boy grown to manhood in the company of a father or uncle who was a leader learned more about the business of leadership and as he became an adult gradually assumed the role. The Washo view that most successful human actions were the result of supernatural assistance and their feeling that power seemed to concentrate in certain families probably encouraged this succession of leadership. However, the Washo kinship system in which a person traced his descent in both the patrilineal and matrilineal lines allowed for a variety of claimants for leadership positions to appear.

The Washo, however, did not seek responsibility for the acts or decisions of others. Power, it was felt, was thrust on a person and was an uncomfortable and in some cases dangerous burden. As often as not, a man would seek to escape the responsibility of leadership which he seemed destined by descent to assume and some other person, more aggressive or willing, would take his place. A particularly forceful woman, especially an older woman, might assume the leadership and direction of a bunch if no man appeared to become leader. There is also a great deal of evidence that the limits of a particular bunch might expand or contract according to the activity in which it was engaged. Thus, a family was part of a bunch which regularly staged rabbit drives together, but this entire group was considered as part of some other leader's bunch in the event of a war party or antelope drive or girl's dance.

Although we have seen that kinship was not an all important factor in who lived with what bunch, or in fact who might become part of a household, the kinship system of the Washo was not unimportant in their lives. Indeed an understanding of the principles of Washo kinship helps shed some light on the dynamics of the family and the bunch.

Kinship

The basic principle of Washo kinship reckoning was bilaterality, that is, an individual Washo considered relatives of his mother and father as being related to him equally. This principle is similar to that observed in our own society but in distinct contrast with the practice in many societies. There are many examples of peoples who feel more closely related to one side of their descent than to the other. If the father's side is considered closest, the system is termed patrilineal. If the mother's side is felt to be closest, the society is called matrilineal. Societies of either type are called unilineal. Unilineal kinship systems often place rather specific strictures on the responsibilities and obligations of one relative to another. Such restrictions are clearly incompatible with the demands of Washo environment which requires a flexible and rather opportunistic pattern of human behavior if the human group is to survive. Thus we find the bilateral principle to be common throughout the Great Basin and indeed other parts of the world where human beings attempt to exploit a hostile environment with a simple technology.

Some fifty-four different kinship terms used by the Washo have been reported. An analysis of the entire system of terms is too complex an undertaking for this book. It is important to know, however, that the Washo distinguish their siblings by relative age so that there are separate terms for older brother and younger brother, older sister and younger sister. These terms are extended to cover the children of one's mother's and father's siblings as well, so there is no distinct term for cousin as there is in English. Words related to the sibling terms are used to refer to and address distinct relatives or friends whose closeness places them within a network of fictitious kinship relations and obligations. The largest number of terms is found in a class used by persons toward their grandparents and to their grandchildren. The children of the children of one's siblings are carefully distinguished. Special terms are used for father's mother's sisters and mother's mother's sisters who stand in the relation of a kind of extra grandparent. A number of terms occur to describe the relationship between a boy and his parent's brothers, the uncle-nephew relationship being particularly important. None are reported for the parent's sister, this being a rather unimportant relationship in Washo life. In addition to blood or consanguineal relationship terms, a number of special terms are used to describe relatives by marriage. Parents-in-law are recognized as are the spouse's siblings. The husbands and wives of one's parent's siblings are not considered relatives and no terms exist to describe this relationship. While the terms in one's own generation and that of his parents and grandparents carefully distinguish sex and often whether maternal or paternal, one term is used to cover all relatives of a third ascending generation or, as we would say, great grandparents. Similarly, there is only a single term for a great-grandparent to use toward a great-grandchild no matter which sex or in what manner descended.

All societies avoid as a moral imperative marriages between close relatives. In large complex societies such as our own, this presents very little problem inasmuch as the large population offers many opportunities to find unrelated persons to marry. In smaller societies living in fairly close proximity, the possibility of two persons being biologically related is greatly increased. Among many peoples, the Washo included, it is possible to trace the actual biological relationship of any two persons. This presents a problem in the avoidance of incest unless relationships are defined in such a way that the problem does not arise. Kinship systems are not then actual descriptions of biological relationships but rather systems used to describe socially approved and significant relationships. In unilineal societies a husband and wife must belong to different descent groups. Their children will belong to either the husband's group or the wife's group which will define the limits of incest. Thus marriage with a mother's brother's child would be approved in a matrilineal society because he or she would not be of the same descent group as your own mother or her brother. In unilineal systems large classes of people can be automatically excluded as possible partners and other large classes are automatically included simply by reference to the system of unilineal descent, without consideration of what the actual biological relationship may be. The problem is solved by the Washo by ignoring relationships past the third ascending or descending generation. All relatives three generations removed are called by the same term. In the next generation there is no term at all. Therefore, a boy and a girl with the same great-grandparent could not marry because they both called the same person *dipisew*. But, if they had the same great great-grandparent and no common relatives after that, they would be considered unrelated and thus able to marry.

Kinship does more than determine who may or may not marry. In Washo life where the vagaries of the environment may at any time force a person to seek assistance from his fellows, relationships are exceedingly important. We have seen that there are a great many people classed as siblings, that is, people of one's own generation whose life cycle will closely parallel your own. In times of emergency, siblings real or fictive can be expected to help one another, and if one person called brother or sister is unable to help, there are many others to whom a person can turn. Similarly, a grandparent must increasingly depend on his children's children for support in his old age. It is here that we see a large number of kinship terms defining the relationship between a person three generations removed from another and providing a great number of opportunities for an old person to seek assistance. Given the relatively brief life span of primitive peoples it is highly unlikely that a great-grandchild would be old enough to provide assistance to a great-grandparent, a situation which appears to be reflected by the single catch-all term for that relationship.

The individual Washo is embedded in a network of kinsmen and has at his disposal numerous terms of reference for each kind of relative. Along these lines of relationship he can seek assistance in hunting or war or courtship. He can refer to his relationship with some member of a household if he should seek to take up residence outside his own home or find a host should he be traveling. If he seeks to join another bunch, it is probable that among its members will be someone, perhaps several people, to whom he can refer as a close relative. Should this not be the case, he can call close friends by a sibling term or apply the sibling term to the most distant of relatives. Washo environment demanded a flexible system so that the individual and his family could survive and the Washo kinship system met those demands admirably. Even a complete stranger entering a group would, unless personal animosity developed to drive him out, soon become classed as a sibling or friend and thus become part of the network of kinsmen. As we examine other aspects of Washo social organization, we can see how kinship, subsistence activity, and the environment interacted to create social institutions significant beyond the level of the family and the local bunch.

Regional Groups or "Moieties"

An individual's identification with a bunch or even with a family household was impermanent and quite apt to change in the course of his life. There was, however, a broader level of organization with which a Washo individual was more permanently, but not irrevocably, connected. Some anthropologists have called this a moiety system, that is, a division of the Washo people into two parts. However, in most societies which display moiety organization, the divisions play a much more important role than they did among the Washo. Many anthropologists believe that larger divisions of Washo social organization cannot be properly considered as moieties but as a reflection on Washo "ethnogeography," that is, the way the Washo viewed and identified the land in which they lived.

Washo territory was divided into four major sections: the west, or *tangelelti;* the east, or *pauwalu;* the north, or *welmelti;* and the south, *hanelelti.* People were given an identification with a region based on the location of their winter camp, or *galesdangl.* Inasmuch as the west or *tangelelti* was in the mountains and subject to heavy snows, few, if any, people wintered there so there were no people identified with this area. Because the Washo could and did move frequently on their hunting and gathering rounds and often changed bunches, set up new homes and allied themselves with different households, it was possible for a person identified with one zone to establish a home in another. The tendency seems to have been for a person to remain in the general area in which he had been born. Most "southerners" then remained "southerners" all their lives, associating with the same people and interacting with their kinsmen. Such a situation makes these regional divisions appear more permanent and kin-based than they actually were. Persons designated by the same regional term were not considered kinsmen and there was no restriction on their marrying if they were not otherwise related. When marriages were contracted between persons from different regions, one of the spouses usually changed his or her designation to that of the marriage partner.

At large gatherings such as the spring fishing around Lake Tahoe and the *gumsaba,* people from the various regions camped together. In the spring, the northerners tended to camp along the northern shore of the lake, the southerners on the south, and the easterners on the eastern shore. This seems more of a convenience then an adherence to any rule, inasmuch as the various parts of the huge lake were simply closer to the winter camps in the various regions. At the *gumsaba* the large camp was formed in a circle with the various divisions each occupying part of the arc. There is some question as to whether any such large-scale gathering occurred in aboriginal times. In fact, the social usages surrounding these area designations may have been a result of the closer association of the Washo from various parts of the country after the white man's appearance had made great changes in Washo life. There is evidence of hostility between the "northerners" and the "southerners" which is displayed even today. Conflicting claims to the "chiefdomship" of all the Washo spring up in both areas and many traditional tales tend to suggest that northern Washo were considered as strangers by the southern groups.

When the tribe did come together, these regional divisions formed the basis for choosing sides in games and races, the northerners against the southerners with the easterners dividing themselves between the two. However, regional ties were so light that a man participating in the team gambling games that were so popular with the Washo would move to the other team in order to change his luck. One might ask why, if the regional divisions played such a small part in Washo life, they were important at all? Perhaps the reason that they are worth discussing is what they can teach us about social organization on such a simple technological level. And, despite their superficiality, these identifications were and are regularly used by the Washo themselves. They can probably be understood best if we examine the dynamics of a hunting and gathering culture in this kind of an environment.

The animal on which the Washo depended for a major source of their food, the deer, live in small herds and are particularly wary and difficult to hunt. Even with firearms, a successful hunter must know more than just how to use his weapon; he must have more than a general knowledge of forest lore. To be really successful, an intimate knowledge of a particular region is required. A hunter must understand the habits of his quarry, not in general, but in a highly specific way. Game trails, springs, and salt licks, favorite browsing areas and bedding places, the behavior of scent in certain areas and an understanding of the prevailing winds and the behavior of animals under certain microclimatic conditions are essential to a successful hunt, the more so if the hunter must approach his quarry within a few feet. To learn this requires many years of training, beginning in early childhood. Even the most successful hunter moving into a strange area would not be much better than the newest tyro until he knew the new area as well as he had known his previous hunting grounds. Thus, among most peoples who hunt game of this sort, there is a distinct economic advantage for a man to remain within the area where he has been raised. This is the area in which his grandfather, father, and uncles have taught him the business of hunting. In this way a bias toward the paternal side of one's family tends to develop. When a man marries, he sets up his own household in his home area. Inasmuch as people from a single region tend to see each other more frequently than people from different regions, there is a tendency for a young man to marry a woman of his home region. In this way, quite without reference to any over-all rules of kinship, several generations of a bilateral family may include only persons born and raised in a single region. This gives the appearance of kinship based units, although the basic factors involved have little to do with kinship reckoning. Nonetheless, these divisions did have meaning to the Washo and formed the conceptual basis for identifying groups of people within the totality of the Washo "tribe."

The Tribe

One of the most difficult terms to define precisely is the word "tribe." It has, in modern America, come to have a specific legal definition, but this helps us very little in attempting to understand the political organization of aboriginal populations. In some parts of pre-Columbian America, societies were organized in such a manner that Europeans could equate them with political units in the Old World. Leadership roles were clearly defined and the political rights and obligations were understood by all the members of the group or tribe. In the Great Basin, however, political institutions were weak, if not almost nonexistant, and nowhere were they less developed than among the Washo. Certainly there was no over-all chief or leader for all the Washo in aboriginal times. Even the distinction of language and culture, which served to delimit some many separate groups in aboriginal America, were vague. Along the edges of the Washo country, where there was a great deal of interaction between the Washo and their Paiute neighbors, bunches or bands existed in which intermarriage was so common as to cause them to be identified as "half Paiute" by the Washo. Leadership within the local bunches and in the loose alliances of a number of bunches was informal and transitory. A leader gave advice and counsel but there seems to have been no compulsion to obey. Temporary leaders of rabbit hunts, antelope drives, and deer hunting expeditions had authority to direct those activities but their power was limited and specific to the event. While a reputation as a successful antelope boss or rabbit boss might enhance a man's general reputation for leadership, it was no gaurantee that his wishes would prevail save perhaps among his immediate relatives.

Disputes between individuals or between families were not referred to any body of law but were settled according to an established code of conduct. Thus, if a man found a stranger trespassing on his pine nut plot, he seized his equipment, broke it, and confiscated the nuts. Inasmuch as this was in accordance with custom, public opinion sided with him and the matter was settled because the trespasser could not get support among his neighbors. Men might come to blows over the use of a fishing platform but here again custom established who had prior rights and if custom was followed, public opinion was not roused. Disputes over food were relatively rare as generosity and sharing were primary Washo virtues. A hunting party divided its take equally and assistance in any task automatically meant that a debt had been incurred which had to be repaid in goods, food, or services, either then or in the future. Failure to act generously brought down the disapproval of one's neighbors and threatened the miser with a withdrawal of assistance which was tantamount to a sentence of death or, at the least, pauperism. All of these things were carried out without formal courts or even public judgment of the "crime." In serious disputes between individuals there was always the possibility of a feud developing. Vengeance could be taken by killing one's antagonist. If this was done, the enemy was ambushed and killed. The act was kept secret by the killer and his family, because retaliatory killings could be expected if the killer's identity became known. Such feuds were relatively rare. Washo existence was too precariously perched on the foundation of a not always provident environment to permit the luxury of unrestrained feuding. The threat of schisms which would effect the cooperation of groups or even limit the mobility of groups in search of food was sufficient to inhibit murder and retaliation save under the most extreme circumstances.

While Washo custom worked to prevent hostilities and serious conflict within the tribe, it was necessary to contend with the aggressive acts of strangers and to protect the heartland of the Washo territory from unwanted intrusions. It is in this circumstance, action against foreigners, in which the Washo acted most like a single unit. The Paiute to the east and the Maidu and Miwok to the west were constant threats to the resources of the Washo country. People living near the boundaries of Washo territory were constantly on the alert for signs of raiding parties. If intruders were bent on peaceful activities, to trade or to gather vegetable food, the Washo did not interfere. Even hunting parties appear to have sometimes been allowed to hunt unmolested in what the Washo considered their own land.

The Washo were not a warlike people and their response to the presence of strangers was generally to withdraw and observe them until their intentions were clear. Washo bands inhabiting the border regions kept a constant vigil against encroachment. Washo tradition holds that certain lookout posts were always manned, although this seems unlikely. If the intruder's intentions seemed hostile, or it appeared that they intended to trespass on forbidden ground, the Washo would attack. The most common tactic was an ambush, preferably of the enemy camp at night. The weapon was usually the bow, using special large war arrows which are said by some to have been rubbed with a mixture of secret ingredients to effect instant death.

Occasionally, more formal battles appear to have been fought. Washo tales of using stone to build crude breastworks behind which they could stand and fire at their attackers are frequent. Older Washo informants, recalling the tales of their grandparents, stress the defensive nature of Washo warfare. They recite what is almost a litany of battlegrounds where the invasions of Paiute from the east and the California tribes from the west were resisted. The places mentioned form a definite boundary around the core of the Washo country. However, all Washo warfare was not purely defensive and there are traditions of aggressive raids particularly to the west against the Miwok or the Maidu or, as the Washo call them, "the Diggers." These raids appear to have been retaliatory in nature. The only goal was to inflict death and wounds on their enemies. When such an enterprise was planned, the leader of the bunch which originated the idea would send a messenger to leaders throughout the Washo country asking for assistance. The messenger carried with him the familiar deer hide thong with a knot to mark each day before the expedition was to march. Each day he untied a knot. The summons was not necessarily a command and no one was compelled to join the war party. In certain areas the Washo were famed for their "roughness," that is their willingness to enter into any kind of a fray. The people living in the area of Woodfords and Markleville, California, were always sought by other Washo because of their reputation for bravery, reckless courage, and some supernatural power in war. Other bands were equally famous for non-violence and seldom joined raiding parties.

Full-scale war parties of this type disappeared soon after the appearance of whites in the area and much of the ritual and ceremony surrounding war is now forgotten. There was a period of perhaps as long as a month during which warriors prepared for battle by dancing and praying but the exact nature of the ceremony is now lost. Warriors bedecked themselves in close-fitting hats covered with magpie feathers. A powerful and famous warrior might suspend an eagle feather from the top of his hat and, if he owned enough feathers, one from each of his upper arms. The Washo did not have any special war magic, but they did believe that the Maidu to the west were able to cast a spell over an enemy village and put everyone to sleep. The return from a successful raid was also the occasion for a ceremony but this too is all but forgotten. Old informants recall hearing descriptions of the dance honoring a returning war party and insist that the ritual included the use of a single scalp taken from the enemy. Another dance performed frequently during the 1890's in the Woodfords area and in the Sierra Valley area was called a "war dance" by both whites and Washo but appears to have nothing to do with warfare. The acquisition of the horse and firearms by the northern Paiute bands upset the military balance between them and the Washo. In response, the Washo abandoned attempts to resist Paiute intrusions and instead withdrew into the mountains and avoided contact wherever possible. The long-term consequences of this altered situation can never be determined because the new Paiute strength coincided with appearance of the white man and the diversion of Paiute efforts into unsuccessful attempts to resist the latter.

Hostilities were always a threat to Washo who moved outside of the center of Washo territory. Hunting parties traveling west and families coming into California to gather pine nuts usually camped without fires once they crossed the divide of the Sierra Nevada. After they had made overtures to the inhabitants of the area, they might be accepted into the village and remain there, eventually even intermarrying, but while they were traveling and until their intentions were clear they might be attacked. Hunting parties considered it an omen of a forthcoming attack if the meat drying rack fell to the ground. If this happened, they quickly decamped and went into hiding. This habit of caution while outside Washo territory was maintained well into this century, although intertribal war had disappeared and hostilities had been reduced to shouting insults and rock throwing. Although it is certain that on occasion Washo from various areas banded together to raid the enemy or defend themselves, it is doubtful that the entire population of warriors ever joined in a single expedition. People in the north tended to cooperate with each other, as did people in the south, but it was not until the appearance of the white man that the entire tribe ever joined in any united action.

The information on warfare illustrates the weak development of any political consciousness of a Washo tribe as a whole. While the Washo clearly differentiated between themselves and all other peoples, using various cultural criteria, it is clear that they felt no over-all obligations simply because of this relationship. War was one of the mechanisms for dealing with non-Washo people, but it was generally a local matter resorted to resolve local problems and not considered a "nation-wide" affair.

Peaceful Relations

As often as the Washo might fight with their neighbors, they had other contacts with the same tribes. We have described trade as one such relationship. Another was mentioned in the previous section. The Washo striking west to hunt or gather often chose to spend the winter in the villages of their hosts and erstwhile enemies. Many intermarriages are recorded and Washo men frequently brought back foreign brides. One of the reasons given for the fierceness of the men in the Woodfords area was the amount of Miwok blood in their veins. Reciprocal trips by the Californians to the east appeared to have been less frequent but not altogether lacking. With intermarriage relatively common, it was possible to extend the network of kinship relations beyond the tribe in finding "relatives" among foreigners. As was so common in Washo life, these "international" relations were a matter of family, bunch, or, at best, local band concern. The institutionalized social units of Washo society were few and thus had to serve many purposes.

In this section we have seen how the Washo organized themselves into groups to solve the problems of subsistence and interpersonal and intertribal relations. One other major aspect of Washo life deals with the way the Washo handled the problem of dealing with the supernatural.

6

Spirits, Power, and Man

WITHIN THE SCOPE of his limited technology, the Washo was a rational person, well aware of cause and effect and prepared to handle the exigencies of his position. However, the precarious balance of Washo society often made survival seemingly dependent on chance. Why should a well-trained hunter locate his quarry only to have it escape him at the last moment? How could a well-made and well-aimed arrow miss an easy shot? Why should one man on a raid be wounded or killed and another escape unscathed? Why should the pine nut tree be fruitful one year and not at all the next? How was it that sickness struck down one person and passed over another? Why indeed should a man, unwounded and unhurt, die at all? These questions plague all societies and in many, including our own, are more or less successfully resolved in sophisticated theologies. Among many primitives, the basis of religion is an explanation of both the how and the why of the vagaries of life. The ritual of many primitive peoples, including those of the Washo, are both expressions of the Washo view of cause and effect and an attempt to maintain an understandable order to life.

The Washo did not articulate a complete philosophy or theology. Their religious life dealt with the practical day-to-day events: hunting, war, love, birth, health, and death. Yet we can present an organized picture of Washo religious life. We must remember, however, that a systematic presentation of Washo religion is a device which helps us understand a foreign and confusing point of view. It does not reflect the minds of the Washo as they go about their daily tasks, scarcely separating the sacred and the profane.

Power

To many of the questions posed above the Washo's answer was "power." A successful hunter was more than skilled and careful, he was aided by a special power. A man who dreamed of rabbits or antelope was more than simply lucky, he was a possessor of a special power. The nature of this power is not clearly defined in all cases. We can see how power works most clearly if we learn how a man becomes a "doctor," or shaman, among the Washo. The shaman was expected to carry his share of the burden of living, but his special powers set him apart from his fellows and contributed to his livelihood because his services were valuable and demanded payment. The shaman's special power was the ability to diagnose and cure illness.

Illness might come from three sources. A ghost, angry because some piece of his property was being used by the living, might make the user sick. A sorcerer might cause illness by using magic to "shoot" a foreign body into his victim. Or a person might become ill because he had violated some taboo such as mistreating pine nuts or piñon trees. To affect a cure, a shaman was called to perform a ceremony over the patient. The cure was felt to be brought about not by the shaman's skill but by his "power" which was felt to be apart from the person of the shaman himself. The shaman served as a medium through which the power could be used to the benefit of the sick person. A treatment required that the shaman work for four nights. In addition to the shaman, the patient's family and a number of friends gathered. On each of the nights the shaman prayed to his power to assist him, smoked tobacco, frequently a sacred or semi-sacred act among Indians; and sang special songs which were his alone. Accompanying his singing with a rattle made of dry cocoons, he passed into a trance and while in this state located the site of the illness and identified the cause. If a ghost was the cause, the shaman would identify the contaminating object and instruct the patient as to whether he should get rid of it or perhaps simply treat it differently. If, on the other hand, an enemy had "shot" a sickness into the patient, the shaman would remove it by sucking, employing an eagle feather and tobacco smoke to make the extraction easier. When the object was removed and shown to the patient and his guests, the shaman would lecture it and then throw it away into the night. He was able to produce an object by means of legerdemain. He did not, however, feel that this was in any way hypocritical. His ability to perform these slight-of-hand tricks was part of the exercise of his power. We might compare his use of slight-of-hand to instill confidence in his power to the bedside manner of a modern doctor attempting to instill confidence in his patients. For his services a shaman was paid in food and valuable objects. The process of becoming a doctor illustrates the nature of power as the Washo conceived it.

The power to become a shaman was not sought by the Washo, it came unsought and often unwelcomed. The first signs of receiving power were often a series of dreams. In these dreams an animal, a bear, an owl, a "ghost" or some other being would appear. The vision would offer him power and assistance in life. The Washo feared power; it was dangerous for one who had it and the greater and more clearly defined the power, the more dangerous it was. The trancelike state which was part of the curing ceremony seemed to many Washo to be akin to death, a loss of spirit. Because of this, a young man might ignore the offers of spiritual power. But a spirit being, or *wegaleyo,* frequently refused to be ignored. It would begin to inflict a series of ailments upon its chosen vehicle. Although it was not considered good social form to brag of having power or to openly seek it, some men did secretly hope for power. Men of this type today invariably complain of a long series of illnesses, seizures, and ailments. To the outsider such a person might appear to be simply a hypochondriac, but the Washo recognized this as a veiled claim to power. Under pressure from the *wegaleyo,* a man would usually succumb and accept his power. Once he had made this secret decision, his dreams would become instruction sessions. The *wegaleyo* would tell him where he could find a special spring or pool. This was "his water" to be used in ceremonies or for ritual bathing or to decontaminate sacred articles collected by the shaman in his career. The spirit also taught his pupil a special song which he would remember word for word when he awoke. In later years a shaman might learn many such songs from his spirit. He would also receive instructions as to what equipment to collect. This would always include a rattle and eagle feathers. Individuals might also possess special stones, shell jewelry, or animal skins. These objects were usually obtained under unusual or miraculous circumstances. One shaman, for instance, had a stone shaped like a human molar which attracted his attention by whistling until he located the stone. In addition to his instructions direct from his spirit, a prospective shaman would seek out an established practitioner and apprentice himself to the older man. The tutor would instruct his apprentice in the arts of legerdemain, ventriloquism, and such feats as smoking several pipefulls of tobacco without allowing the smoke to escape from his lungs. In time, after his powers were known through participation in ceremonies held by his mentor, a shaman would be asked to perform cures of his own.

Shamans were always considered to be potential sorcerers. Their power was neither good nor bad in itself and could be used for whatever ends the shaman sought. The ability to use power against others is illustrated in a traditional Washo tale, which also points out the basic suspicion held by southern Washo toward northern Washo. According to the story, a northern Washo appeared at a camp in Carson Valley and there asked for food. Because he was a stranger, he was refused by all but one old woman. She fed the stranger and allowed him to sleep in her camp. The man left the camp determined to work vengeance on the people who had been so miserly with him. Walking west from Carson Valley, the northerner rested at the hot springs near Markleville. There performing some unknown magic, he pointed his finger in the direction of the camp. The power he controlled killed all the members of the camp, save the old woman who had been generous to him. Modern Washo insist that one can see a barren line in the earth stretching from Markleville to Carson Valley. They also insist that the campsite is covered with skeletons and abandoned equipment. This winter camp may well have been struck by the plague or some other epidemic disease.

Tradition describes other uses of shamanistic power. In what might be described as advertising contests, shaman engaged in tests of power, particularly at gatherings such as the *gumsaba.* The most common demonstration of power was said to be setting a number of stakes in a line. The shaman would point at the sticks and the winner of the contest was the shaman who could knock down the most sticks. Shaman are reported to have engaged in casual displays of power by offering an unsuspecting victim a pipe, or in later times, a cigarette. The shaman's power would remain in the pipe or cigarette and the smoker would be knocked flat or perhaps unconscious. To possess such power was dangerous and inconvenient. A person who received his power from the deer, for instance, could no longer eat deer meat. If he did, he would become ill and perhaps die. The possession of power also made one subject to frightening and mysterious experiences. A well-known shaman in the early part of this century staged a curing ceremony during which he fell into the fire while in a trance. Burning his trousers off, he had to go home wearing his shirt as a loin cloth although he was not hurt. On his way the shaman stopped at a stream to bathe. As he bent over the water, he fell into a faint and was taken down into the water. There he was greeted by Water Baby, a spirit creature said to inhabit all bodies of water in the Washo country. The Water Baby took the shaman into a strange land to meet the king of the Water Babies who lived in a large stone house. There the shaman was entertained by five young girls who taught him a special song. The Water Baby guide then took the shaman back to the surface and left him where the frightened man awoke floating in the water.

If a shaman lost his sacred paraphernalia or it was destroyed, he would most certainly become seriously ill. Because of these dangers, many men tried to avoid power if it was thrust upon them and would employ a shaman to help them rid themselves of the persistent spirit. If this was successful they could resume the normal Washo life. If not, they had little choice but to quiet the spirit and accept its gift.

The nature of power is most clearly seen in the complex of Washo shamanism, but *wegelayo* often provided special powers of a less general nature. Some men with a water *wegelayo* were believed to be able to bring rain. Others who had been visited by the bear *wegelayo* might on accasion act like a bear and be particularly brave or notably short tempered. Others might have the power to handle rattlesnakes with impunity and cure rattlesnake bites. The Water Baby might act as a *wegelayo* and give a person the power to walk under water. There is said to be a broad road of white sand across the bottom of Lake Tahoe. This was the special route of men with Water Baby *wegelayo* who wished to visit the beds of wild poison parsnips on the north shore of the lake. These poison plants used to be eaten with impunity as a demonstration of power. Some specially powerful men received their power from a number of different sources all of which helped in curing or performing other miracles.

The most dangerous task for a shaman was to recover the soul of a person who had apparently died. It was believed that with the help of his *wegelayo* a shaman could go into a trance and, in spirit form, follow the soul of the dead person into the land of the dead. This was described as a place in the sky to the south of Washo country. Its approaches were guarded by a number of fierce warriors. Behind these sentries was a spring. If the shaman could overtake the soul before it had drunk from the spring he could return it to its earthly body and revive his patient. This land of the dead was said to be a happy place where people played games and gambled and danced unless they had committed a murder. Murderers were banned by the other shades and placed in a kind of heavenly coventry.

We have spoken of shaman as being males, but women could also become shaman and many did. Their experiences and training did not differ from those of men. Power was not exclusively a gift of the spirit beings to humans. In a general way, everything was viewed as having some power. Merely to live required some supernatural assistance. Successful survival was a sign of power and thus old people had demonstrated that they were powerful. There was a widespread belief that old people were dangerous and should not be offended or harmed lest they retaliate by using their power. This belief worked to assure that an ancient Washo in his final years would receive support from those who were obligated to him. Even though he might be unable to share the burdens of life, he could avenge himself on those who did not behave ethically. This general power was extended to all living things, animals, and plants and, as we have seen, was the basis of many of the behavior patterns associated with hunting, fishing, and gathering.

Ghosts

The spirits of the dead were to be greatly feared and avoided. No Washo ever thought of his ancestors as benign figures concerned with his happiness and welfare. Instead they were angry and vengeful. If their property was used or misused, is their burial was not properly conducted, or for any one of a dozen other sins of ommission or commission, the dead might return to plague the living. Therefore Washo funerals were not ceremonies designed to honor the dead or comfort the living. They were ways of making sure the dead person's spirit would not return. It was for this reason that his home was burned or abandoned. If he returned to familiar haunts, the house and family would be gone. For the same reason his clothing and personal property were burned or buried with him. A person using some possession of a dead man was always liable to a visit from the ghost who had located his property and found the user. The brief Washo burial prayers were really exhortations to the dead person to accept his death and leave the living alone. He was told that no one had killed him and that no one was angry at him. Association with the dead was slightly contaminating and upon returning from funerals people washed themselves before handling food or touching children lest the contamination spread and attract the ghost. The Washo argue that it is the nature of things that the dead should remain dead and not bother the living. For this reason they say a rain storm always occurs after a death to wipe out the footprints of the deceased and thus remove all traces of his existence. The taboo on using the name of the dead was another such precaution. Despite all these precautions, the dead did return. Sometimes they came on specific missions of vengeance and on other occasions to simply wander in the vicinity of human beings. The twirling dust devils so common in the summer in this region were thought to be ghosts, and a sudden puff of warm air on a still summer night was most certainly a shade. The belief in ghosts and personal power was an important factor in Washo child raising practices. Parents avoided striking or spanking or striking a child for fear of angering some dead relative. In this instance the ghost seemed to have some friendly concern for the living, but the manner of showing it was to cause the death of the child as a punishment to the parents. The fear of sorcery led the Washo to encourage their younger children to remain within their own family group. Associating with strangers, particularly old strangers, could be dangerous. This belief is obviously related to the development of deep ties of dependence on one's close relatives and the strengthening of the all important Washo family unit. The two major concepts of Washo religion are: ghosts, to be feared, avoided, and appeased; and power, to be used to accomplish the business of living. But, these were not all the facets of Washo religion. Like most people the Washo had explanations for the natural and human environment in which they found themselves. These explanations were preserved in a body of mythology. The corpus of myth was not an elaborate and involved body of scripture. Rather, it consisted of a number of rather simple tales, many of which seem confused and inconsistent to foreigners.

Creation

Two myths deal with creation and although they are quite different, the inconsistency seems not to trouble the Washo who use whichever set of tales seems most appropriate at the time. The world is described in one set of myths as having gone through a number of stages. In each stage there was a different set of inhabitants, the modern Indians representing the fifth inhabitation of the earth. The creation of the various cultural groups known to the Washo is attributed to "Creation Women" who made the Washo, the Paiutes, and the Diggers (a generic term for California Indians) out of the seeds of the cattail. Still another tale tells of how a different personage, "Creation Man," formed the three groups by separating his three sons so they would not quarrel. The natural features of the Washo country are usually explained by reference to a pair of weasels. These two, *Damalali* (short-tailed weasel) and *Pewetseli* (long-tailed weasel), traveled together. The wiser *Pewetseli* usually managing to save the day threatened by the impulsive behavior of the rascal *Damalali*. The general structure of these tales is reminiscent of a common theme of adventuresome twin brothers found throughout much of western North America. The many lakes in the mountain region are, for instance, said to be caused by one such misadventure of the weasels. *Damalali,* the story says, came upon a Water Baby and took it prisoner. The water creature at first begged for his freedom and finally threatened to flood the world. When neither pleading nor threats moved the weasel, the Water Baby made good his threat and caused a flood to come which covered the mountains to their tips. *Pewetseli,* furious at his companion's irresponsibility, forced him to release the water spirit and begged the creature to lower the waters. This the Water Baby did, but in every mountain valley a lake remained. The adventures of this pair are seemingly endless, many of the incidences are virtually meaningless to the outsider, and in many cases the modern Washo appear to have forgotten the real significance of the episode. In other cases they appear to be simply humorous or sometimes salacious stories told for amusement.

Other Figures

A number of other miraculous figures appear in Washo mythology, all of them threatening and dangerous at least in part. *Hanglwuiwui,* a great one-eyed, one-legged giant, is said to have hopped from hilltop to hilltop in search of his favorite food, Indians. Near Gardenerville, Nevada, there is a cave called by the Washo *Hanglwuiwuiangl,* the dwelling of Hanglwuiwui, which is still avoided or approached with caution, although most Washo say that the giant has been dead for a long time.

Another fearsome feature of Washo mythology was the *Ang,* a great bird which carried off human victims and terrorized the world. Birds such as this figure in many Indian myths. The *Ang* is said to have died and fallen into Lake Tahoe where its skeleton formed a reef, which the Washo insist can be seen by anyone flying over the lake. The failure of white airplane pilots to report the reef is felt to be a conspiracy to discredit Washo belief.

The coyote, a figure found almost universally in Indian mythology, was prominent in Washo legends. As is true in other tribes, the nature of coyote is exceedingly difficult to define. In some episodes he is a dangerous and threatening force, in others quite benevolent, and in yet others a rather stupid fellow given to jokes and tricks and generally finding himself the laughing stock. One such tale describes the coyote attempting to seduce a young woman who thwarts him by inserting a seed pot between her legs and injuring coyote in an embarrassing and painful manner. Most coyote tales still told emphasize his lecherous and rascally nature and are told as salacious stories rather than moral fables. Some persons were felt to be able to turn themselves into coyotes and threaten their fellow men. Stories of such occurences are not unknown today.

In addition to the one-legged giant, the Washo believed that the mountains were inhabited by another race, possibly human but possessed of much more power than ordinary people. These giants or wild men figure in many stories of disappearance or mysterious occurences while on hunting trips. Occasionally, they directly attacked humans, trying to steal food from them or otherwise bother them. In most cases in stories dealing with these direct confrontations, the wild man was bested by the cleverness or courage of the Washo. In 1911 an Indian appeared in Oroville, California, attempting to steal scraps from a local slaughterhouse. He was eventually identified as Ishi, the last survivor of a small band of southern Yana who had maintained a furtive and fearful freedom in the Sierra foothills. His appearance caused a minor sensation as the "last wild Indian" in the United States. Modern Washo believe that he was not an Indian but one of the wild men of their myths.

One Washo tale tells of a great battle between the Washo and the giants in which the giants, who had no bows, were defeated after building a fort and throwing stones at the Washo. It is possible that the wild men represent some previous culture inhabiting the region. References to them and to a great battle in which they were exterminated are found in the mythologies of many groups in the Great Basin. Many of the Washo myths have been forgotten or have become garbled as the Washo world changed and the conditions that they have described and explained disappeared. One figure has maintained its vitality and dominates the supernatural life of the modern Washo as it did that of the aboriginal tribe. This is the Water Baby mentioned previously. These little creatures are described as being two or three feet tall with long black hair that never touches the ground but instead floats behind the Water Baby when it walks. They are grey in color and soft and clammy to the touch and possess immense power. Every body of water, lake, river, stream, pond, sink, or modern irrigation ditch is occupied by Water Babies. There is, according to Washo tradition, a tunnel from Lake Tahoe to the Carson Valley used by the Water Babies when they travel. All Washo today have heard the high mewing call of the Water Baby luring them toward some body of water at night. When they hear such a summons they hide in their houses and resist the temptation to follow.

In aboriginal times certain springs and lakes were considered to be favorite haunts of the Water Babies. Persons seeking their assistance, in curing an illness for instance, made or purchased an especially fine basket and deposited it in the lake or pond as a gift. Water Baby was a frequent *wegelayo* for the most powerful shamans. As individuals, Water Babies visited human beings. Some Washo believed that simply to see a Water Baby brought illness or death. Others felt it was a good omen, a chance to obtain power. Some others argue that a Water Baby did not give power but instead exchanged it for a human life. A gift of Water Baby was repaid with the life of a relative.

While many of the figures of Washo mythology have grown vague, their stories half forgotten and their place in Washo life reduced, the Water Baby has demonstrated an amazing vitality. Stories of visitations, or hearing Water Baby calls from streams or ponds, of seeing Water Baby footprints are still told. In fact, the Water Baby has kept abreast of the times and one informant with whom I talked stubbornly insisted he could tell a female Water Baby's footprints because she wore high-heeled shoes! Almost all the Washo are somewhat fearful of the consequences of the ignorance of white men in the matter of Water Babies. Fishermen or hunters, they fear, might catch or kill a Water Baby by mistake. One such misadventure is said to have resulted in the San Francisco earthquake of 1906. A fisherman caught a Water Baby and gave it to the San Francisco aquarium. Despite the warnings of a famous Indian leader who went to San Francisco to talk to the mayor, the creature was kept in the aquarium. It remained there until the earth shook and the water came up over the city. When the water receded the Water Baby, of course, was gone.

A most important element of the Washo world was the view that animals were not really any different than human beings. That is, they had societies of their own and languages and a special place in nature and a supernatural power which in some cases was greater than man's. The large and ferocious animals like the bear were considered to be intrinsically more powerful than men and we have seen that to kill a bear was an act which conferred power. Other animals, like men, might or might not have power. But the old buck who successfully eluded the hunter and even a wily rabbit who would not be killed were considered to have special power and to be *mushege* or "wild animals." But the term was not limited to animals alone. A man of particular fierceness or power, one who hunted successfully or was a renowned fighter or who simply had an unpredictable temper, was also called *mushege.* This partial equation of men and animals and the behavior which it engendered, as we shall see, was particularly important in developing the contacts between the Washo and white invaders of their land.

Summary

In this chapter we have examined some of the basic concepts and figures of Washo religious life. Washo religion was not based on a well-developed theological scheme but instead must for the most part be analyzed from the behavior of people in day-to-day life. There were few, if any, purely religious acts. Instead, we see ritual reflecting a Washo view of the supernatural woven through nearly every act of the day. Hunting ritual, dreams of rabbits and fish and antelope, special power to obtain food, respectful treatment of the remains of animals, the minor ceremonies of childbirth and childhood were all viewed as essential parts of the activities with which they were associated. To go hunting without taking the proper ritual steps would be as foolish in Washo eyes as failing to take a bow or using a crooked arrow. To try and hunt with a weapon contaminated by a menstruating woman would be as hopeless as going into the field with a bow but no bowstring. Another feature of Washo religion was that its observance seldom required the participation of specialists or of special groups of people. The ritual of life was the ritual of individuals or individuals within the family group. Certain occasions when people could come together for extended periods were also times when religious rituals were performed. But they were also occasions for games and gambling and courtship and could not be considered purely religious occasions. Even in curing, when a specialist was needed, any shaman would do, if his power was great enough. There was no special caste of priests and any person, man or woman, might become a shaman. Shamans said to have Water Baby power were believed to have a secret cave which could be entered by sinking into Lake Tahoe and then rising inside a great rock. This is the nearest thing to an association or guild of specialists.

In short, Washo religion offered an explanation for the universe as it existed and for the accidents and misadventures of life. It also provided a system of ritual to be used in the business of life which probably allayed some of the fear and uncertainty of the hunting and gathering existence. Because each step in ritual was associated with practical matters, the sacred actions may have provided a framework within which the practical actions could be more easily learned and remembered. As simple as it might be, Washo religion played an important role in aboriginal life and has, as we shall see, a cornerstone of Washo cultural survival in the modern world.

7

California, the Washo, and the Great Basin

IN THE PRECEDING CHAPTERS we have seen how the Washo adjusted their lives to the environment in which they lived, how the one related to the other, and how they felt about and dealt with the supernatural world beyond man's understanding. The Washo world was on the border between two zones of life. To the west were the mountains; green, lake filled, laced with fish-filled streams, falling off into the verdant foothills and valleys of California with its warm summers and mild winters. To the east was the Great Basin; high, arid, covered with dry, quick blooming plants and inhabited by a wide variety of animals. These two life zones were the sites of contrasting systems of culture. The Washo shared in both traditions.

In the Great Basin, all peoples save the Washo spoke languages of the Uto-Aztecan family and practiced a way of life so uniform that it differed only in detail over hundreds of thousands of the arid, inhospitable square miles. In California, the people spoke languages related to every language stock in North America save that of the Eskimo. A wide variety of languages is matched by variations in cultural practices, although language and culture had little correlation. Northwestern California, with its fog-swept mountains plunging to the sea, cut by the Smith, Eel, and Trinity rivers and a hundred lesser streams, was in the zone of Northwest Coast culture which had its center far to the north in Washington, British Columbia, and Alaska. In this area we find speakers of Ritwan, Athapaskan, and Hokan sharing the same general social and cultural configurations. The nearest neighbors of the Washo on the west, southwest, and northwest all spoke dialects of California Penutian, a language stock which dominated an area from the divide of the Sierra west to the Pacific Ocean but was concentrated mainly in the foothills and plains of the great central valleys. These were the acorn Indians, supplied without stint by the millions of oak trees which dotted the area. Moreover, their territory was traced with watercourses. The Sacramento, American, and Feather rivers formed a northern network, the San Joaquin and its tributaries watered the southern zone. Throughout most of this area the salmon came to spawn, entering the inland rivers from the San Francisco Bay where the systems converged. In addition to fish, the foothills and lowlands were rich with game. Deer, antelope, and elk roamed the area in great number. The jack rabbits were plentiful as were other small game animals. The rivers, untapped by irrigation and uncontrolled by dams, flooded in the spring to form huge lakes and swamps which provided homes for dozens of species of waterfowl, geese, ducks, rails, mud hens, and coots. Two varieties of quail lived in the valleys and uplands. And, in addition to the staple acorn, a wide variety of plants provided seeds, roots, and berries. The coast provided fish, sea mammals, shellfish, and crustaceans. Perhaps no place on earth was as consistently provident and hospitable to nonagricultural man as was central California. In contrast to the Great Basin with its low population density, California was the most densely populated area in North America north of agricultural and civilized Mexico.

We know less of southern California in aboriginal times because the Spanish mission endeavors seriously disrupted the aboriginal life. The tribes of southern California have lost, even in their own tongue, identifying words for the aboriginal groups. Instead they are known, save for a few groups in the mountains, by the name of the nearest mission. While not blessed with the water sources found to the north, the southerners still enjoyed a provident environment. There was access to the sea. Some groups lived almost entirely by hunting and fishing on the coast and the coastal islands. The weather was always mild. Deer and jack rabbits were relatively plentiful. Acorns were widely distributed. With more than enough food California Indians were able to live in larger groups. Moreover, they could quite clearly define their territories because a finite zone could supply all the needs of the group. Winter villages were considerably larger than those in the Basin and houses more substantial. Some authorities feel communities of as many as 2000 people existed in ancient California. Houses were often commodious semisubterranean structures. In many areas each village boasted an extremely large house, partially underground, where the men could lounge, sweat in the heat of fires to purify themselves, and in which larger dance gatherings could be held. In the south substantial dwellings of thatch or woven mats replaced the earth houses. The summer was a time of limited wandering and the winter villages were abandoned as the tribe broke up to set up temporary summer camps. Aggressive warfare was almost unknown but the Californians were determined fighters in resisting trespass of their territories. The plentiful supply of food required hard work to collect, but as compared to the Basin, a minimal effort was needed to fill the larder. The Californians had leisure to devote to cultural elaboration. And because they had resources enough for larger groups they also had social problems unknown in the Basin. Larger groups required leaders and a more developed concept of authority. The leisure provided by the environment meant that time was available for the activities of leaders and councils and for ceremonials devoted to the welfare of the entire group. It also meant that within the limits of the technology the creative or ambitious or imaginative Indian had an opportunity to explore and experiment with his or her skills. There was time, for instance, to polish stone cylinders and then painstakingly pierce them from end to end using a sea-lion whisker twisted back and forth in a fine abrasive sand. There was time for women to weave beautiful baskets so small that the stitches can be seen only with a magnifying glass. These tiny baskets had no function save to display the skill of the maker. In the north men worked with obsidian to make huge dou-ble-ended blades, perhaps the finest example of flint knapping in the world, which served no purpose except to enhance the owner's prestige when they were displayed. On the coast and islands of the Santa Barbara area, beautiful bowls were hewn from blocks of soft steatite. The Chumash who inhabited that area made a seagoing plank canoe which has long intrigued ethnologists because the techniques employed are common in the Pacific islands. The dry mountains and desert passes east of the San Bernardino mountains had tribes that knew how to make pottery in which they stored their winter food supplies.

California religious life was varied and complex, far too varied and com-plex to be described in detail. Throughout the state elaborate large scale-ceremo-nies featuring costumed dancers were a part of community life. Puberty rites for boys and girls were more drawn out and complex than those found in the Basin. A form of sand painting was practiced in southern California. The restrictions placed on a young women at the time of her first menses were rigorous and in-volved. Only a society with enough food to allow young women to be totally nonproductive could permit such practices. Young men were initiated in large ceremonies requiring that they drink a concoction made of jimson weed which would produce a vision. Despite the many differences between the tribes and tribe-lets of California, there are certain basic similarities. Death was an obsession. Elaborate funeral ceremonies were held both at the time of death and in annual mourning ceremonies, held a year after the death. Images of the dead person were burned and in southern California the ashes may have been consumed in a drink taken by the mourners. Sweating in special houses to purify themselves before hunting and ceremonial participation was general also. The larger popu-lation and more complex communities of California evolved social structural ele-ments unknown or only vaguely present in the Basin. Many tribes were divided into moieties with clean-cut lines of patrilineal descent. These moieties func-tioned in many contexts, one of them, for instance, having the responsibility for disposing of the dead of the other. This disposal was frequently cremation.

The California tribes observed many of the day-to-day rituals of hunting and interpersonal relations that we have seen among the Washo. But California religion had room for elaboration and there was a tendancy to develop special-ized cults. Animals and birds, particularly the eagle, were taken and kept for a time to be killed and ceremonially interred. An elaborate bird cult was de-veloped in the south-central portion of the state and burials of coyote, bear, bad-ger, and deer have been reported. As specialized cults evolved, so did special-ized shamanism. Among the Washo, we have seen a very weak development of special powers, the average shaman being a general practitioner. In California, shamans were given special power to deal with specific ailments or perform certain miracles. Some were said to be able to turn themselves into bears and they were the most feared. The Californians assumed the responsibility for the world's continuity and annual world renewal ceremonies, held to prevent the world from exploding, were common in many parts of the state. Perhaps this should be expected in an area of frequent earthquakes. This elaboration of religious activities and ceremonials and complexity of social order was reflected in an involved and well-developed body of mythology. The oral literature of the Californians was among the most beautiful and complex in the New World.

There was a tendency among early writers to disregard the achievements of California Indian cultures. Experienced with the farming cultures of the east and the warlike and aggressive tribes of the Great Plains or the well-ordered farming communities of the southwestern pueblos, they gave little notice to the Californians who fought little, seldom wore clothes and when they did, wore very little. This short-sighted view obscured the immense richness of California life. The lack of aggressive behavior is perhaps due to the environment which provided enough, in many cases more than enough, for everyone. Nor were there rich neighbors to tempt the Californians into aggressive actions. To the west was the sea and the east offered only the desert and the Great Basin. Neither external pressures nor internal demands created a need to organize on a larger political scale and form savage kingdoms or tribal alliances. Only along the lower Colorado River where Hokan-speaking tribes with a California culture had learned to farm and also probably had to defend the fertile river lands from envious intruders from the arid lands to the east was war an important activity. Elsewhere in California the defense of tribal territory was the only cause for war and often these disputes were settled by tribal champions while the warriors of the two groups cheered them on.

To some it has seemed odd that, in what is today one of the world's most productive agricultural regions, the Indians had not developed an agricultural tradition. To some it has indicated a lack of ambition and inventiveness among the native Californians. However, we must remember that the very areas of the central valleys which are so productive today were often under water and at the best were swampy. It is doubtful that any people using the techniques of farming known to natives of North America could have produced more food than nature already provided from these areas. Moreover, California is not well suited to the production of maize which requires summer rains and long hot growing periods. Even today maize is a minor feature in California agriculture. The modern productivity of the state is a testimony to advanced technology, irrigation, machine plowing and planting, and vast water control projects. No Indians of the native United States possessed such technical advantages or even knew of the crops which have been most successful in California. In the extreme south, and in the arid mountains lying between San Diego and deserts of the Colorado Basin, where the environment was least provident, some small-scale experimentation with farming was carried out but it was cut short by the changes wrought by white intrusion.

In general, California provided everything man needed for a comfortable life based on hunting and gathering, but it provided no incentive for social and political units larger than the relatively small tribe. Hunting and gathering still placed a premium on the subsistence activities of a family. There was perhaps less need for economic cooperation than in the Basin. Social cooperation was needed to order the life of larger groups but not to support it. This may have been the fatal weakness of the area. When confronted with the intrusion of white men, the California tribes were unprepared and unable to organize a defense. Before they learned the bitter lessons of disunion, it was far, far too late.

While California culture was a picture of primitive life painted in its greatest detail and in its brightest colors, the Basin was life reduced to its simplest elements. Nowhere in the Basin, not even the relatively provident Washo territory, was the land provident enough to support large groups or even semipermanent settlements. All the factors which operated to keep Washo society divided into small independent and mobile units operated even more stringently as one moved east.

In contrast to the multilingual, multicultural nature of California, the Basin was a single entity. All the peoples found there, except the Washo, spoke either a dialect of Paiute or a dialect of Shoshone. The small bands moving regularly wherever food might be found could not defend any permanent territory because they might be forced to move on at any time preventing any attachment to a locality. Thus, there were no elaborate social forms, no moieties or clans or, of course, the ceremonials or ritual associated with such units. Leadership was transitory and informal. Leaders gave advice, not orders, and asked for cooperation instead of demanding it. Whenever an antelope, waterfowl or rabbit drive brought numbers of people together they, like the Washo, held religious and social dances and played group games.

Seldom did these Basin groups engage in warfare. Human life, so difficult to maintain, was not casually risked to defend a plot of pig weed or a grove of piñon trees. Better to move on if the matter could not be settled by argument or by a rock-throwing fight. Better yet, a place already occupied should simply be avoided because it obviously would not support a larger population. If it would, there was no reason for dispute and the two groups could exploit it together and then move on, going their separate ways.

While the Californians enjoyed a rich religious and ceremonial life, the Basin people had a very elementary one. There were shamans, generalists with curing power. Men with the power to dream about antelope and charm them existed and the antelope drive provided the nearest thing to a group ritual and, in many cases, the closest approach to a united political action under a secular leader who was, of course, the shaman. Basin mythology did not involve itself with abstract questions of origins. Simple tales, many of them obscene by our standards, described the adventures of coyote and his brother the wolf, another example of the mythological twins.

Unlike the California tribes, death was not the concern of the Basin tribes. The dead themselves were feared as contaminating and were quickly and fearfully disposed of. No ceremonies of mourning which might call back the ghosts were held.

Basin culture was not rich, Basin society was not involved, and Basin technology was exceedingly simple. Yet we must admire the ability to adjust and adapt which enabled the widely scattered people to live in this inhospitable land. A detailed knowledge of plants and animals and of water sources unknown to white men until recent years and of the cycle of growth in the region enabled the Basin peoples to survive probably far better than it seemed to the first white men who saw them, naked, subsisting on grubs and insects, unhoused and owning nothing more than they could carry. Yet the ability of these people to respond to environmental opportunities is found throughout the Basin. Many groups regularly burned off the brush in the fall and sowed the area with seeds to insure a crop in the spring. Others simply burned away the brush, knowing that it would encourage the growth of seed-producing grasses. In the Owens Valley south of the Washo at the base of the Sierra, groups cooperated in the digging of irrigation ditches to flood meadows where wild grasses grew. Although this practice might have been borrowed from the whites, it formed the basis of relatively permanent and stable communities with regular leaders exercising a degree of authority not known elsewhere in the Basin. In fact, the very simplicity of Basin culture and the need to adapt made it possible for the Paiute and Shoshone to adjust rather rapidly to new opportunities. The horse spread into northern Nevada in the second quarter of the nineteenth century, obtained from the Shoshone and Bannock of the plateau country to the north. The north Paiute quickly adopted the horse and formed Plains Indian-like bands with regular secular chiefs. However, the buffalo was long since gone from the Basin and the Great Plains were hundreds of miles away. The Basin itself provided no species which could be hunted successfully using the horse. Running down the antelope on horseback simply exhausted the supply of these animals that much sooner. The Paiute had little alternative save to turn their mounted war bands against the white newcomers. This raiding led to the wars of the 1850s in which the early successes of the Indians were followed by bloody defeats and a collapse of this short-lived phase of Basin culture.

Between California and the Basin the Washo, separated in language from their neighbors on either side, made their home. The influences of both traditions can be seen in Washo society and culture. A number of anthropologists have called the Washo a California tribe which was pushed over the Sierra and which developed a Basin-like culture.

The environment of Washo country is indeed more Basin-like, a fact clearly reflected in the subsistence cycle and the social organization of the Washo. But there is much of California in Washo culture. It might be likened to a crude water-color imitation, painted on a rough board, of a rich and detailed oil painting done on a well-prepared canvas. Many of the details are gone. The board would not accept the color and the details.

As compared to the Paiute and the Shoshone, Washo mythology was more elaborate. Elements of both the Basin and California can be found, sometimes not too well articulated. For the most part, as we have seen, Washo shamans were generalists but there was a tendency or perhaps a hope of special power. The practice and the opportunity for holding group ceremonials was more common. It is perhaps more important that such observances were expected. Whether or not they were ever really staged, the Washo believed that tribal gatherings were a proper part of life, that some ritual recognition should be given to pine nut harvest and the first fish.

While they did not divide themselves into the clearly demarcated groups which we find in California, there is a sense of permanency and proprietorship about the territorial divisions of the Washo. The traditions of sentries on the border and fights to preserve territorial integrity are more of the California than the Basin tradition. So too are the traditions of war dances and ceremonies before and after a raid. Washo attitudes about death and the dead are more of the Basin, although older informants recall an annual "cry," rather informal and unstructured, which commemorated the dead. If such an observance was made, it was probably borrowed from neighboring tribes and was quickly lost in the changes of the past hundred years. In general, the Washo seemed to look toward California, perhaps we should say back toward their abandoned homeland, for a model on which to base their behavior. Although modern Washo might refer to California tribes as "Diggers," it is clear that they viewed them as rich and powerful and worth imitating. Many of the things the Washo envied simply could not be brought into the Washo environment in aboriginal times. But, as we shall see, the appearance of the white man brought about changes which permitted the Washo to borrow from the Californians. The Washo provide an interesting vantage point from which to view the cultural and social picture of a vast area of the United States stretching from the Rocky Mountains to the Pacific Ocean. Because the history of the Washo since the appearance of the white man in many ways parallels events in both California and the Basin, the examination of this period is an introduction to what is often a sad but still an exceedingly important process, that of acculturation.

8

The White Man and New Alternatives

THE APPEARANCE of Europeans and Africans in the New World after Columbus' voyage set into motion forces which dramatically changed Indian societies and cultures. No matter how remote, no Indian culture survived unchanged when confronted with the pressures of the technically advanced, aggressive, and expanding new American culture. The precise nature of these changes, exactly what elements of non-Indian culture the tribes accepted or rejected, how they responded to new forms of political organizations and new ideas about land ownership and commerce has long been a focus of anthropological interest. This process of borrowing, adapting, and reshaping cultures in prolonged contact has been called acculturation. The term itself has been the center of much scholarly debate and examination. For our purposes we will define the term simply as the study of the changes caused by the intrusion of the Euro-American culture. These changes began almost as soon as Columbus and his men arrived and are continuing even today. Among the last to react to this acculturative process were the scattered people of the Great Basin. The Washo continued to follow their old established patterns well into the nineteenth century and carried them on, with a minimal change, until the twentieth century. In this section we shall examine the past century of relations between the Washo and the foreigners who entered their land and altered the conditions on which Washo life has been based.

Before the First

Historians have carefully combed the records of western exploration in order to establish the precise month and year when the first European entered the Great Basin. It is possible that we will never know absolutely. The mountain men pushing west from the Rockies in search of new beaver country were not all given to writing journals and recording their trips. Nor have we as yet examined all the records of Spanish colonial exploration of the interior. Washo tradition stubbornly holds that Spaniards did cross the Sierra long before the Gold Rush. We do know that many of the earliest travelers in the area were semicriminals who did not leave records of their activities. The first whites to leave a definite record of travel in the Basin were forty trappers who were led by Jedediah S. Smith down the Humboldt River, then to the Walker River, and then following it to its source, crossed into California in 1826.

These early penetrations of the Washo country had no great effect on the Indian way of life. The Washo preferred to watch from a distance and determine what the strangers were up to. Captain John C. Fremont's party, in the 1840s, made contact with several small Washo groups who appeared to be quite frightened. Fremont was distressed by the nearly naked Indians enduring the cold and gave one man some red and blue clothes, the first recorded instance of the Washo receiving material goods from the new culture. Later Fremont employed a Washo as a guide and his presence attracted other Washo who followed the party on their curious round snowshoes. Traditions of the Washo themselves reveal the other side of these first encounters. The stories tell of watching the exploring parties and wagon trains. On one occasion, a cow or ox strayed from an emigrant train and was caught by the Washo. They had observed the travelers well. They packed the ox and led it for a time, then they experimented with riding the beast. Finally they tired of the novelty and butchered the ox and feasted on its flesh. Apparently very little occurred in the Washo country which escaped Indian eyes. During the travail of the Donner party in 1846, the Washo kept the emigrants under surveillance and from time to time left food for the marooned travelers to find. There is a story in the trans-Sierran country that the cannibalism practiced by the Donner party was the reason the Indians were afraid of the whites.

But long before the first sporadic appearance of whites from the east the Washo had been affected by the expansion of the Spanish into California, which made regular trips to the coast for shellfish hazardous. Washo trips into western California became less frequent and more furtive and perhaps stopped altogether. From the southwest, warlike tribes using horses raided into the Great Basin to collect slaves for the markets of Santa Fe and Taos. The first direct contacts between the Washo and white intruders were colored by these earlier experiences. The Washo could be tempted to approach the strangers and receive gifts but the entire relationship was marked with caution.

Before the Rush

The discovery of gold in California in 1848 set off the great migration into the area and many thousands of gold seekers crossed the Washo country enroute to the "diggings." Even before the Gold Rush the tempo of white activity in the Washo country was increasing. Emigrant travel was heavy enough to support a trading post on the Carson River in the vicinity of Woodfords, California. Criminals seeking to take advantage of the emigrants and to avoid even the feeble strength of Spanish law in California established camps on the eastern slope of the Sierra. Travelers usually arrived on the east slope of the mountains with their animals exhausted. The residents of the area would trade fresh animals for the exhausted ones. Usually the animals they traded were obtained from previous parties and grazed into good condition. In addition, there is evidence that they stole great numbers of horses and cattle from the Californians. We have little record of the Washo during this period. The character of the renegades living in the Washo country suggests that they were people with little concern for human life and suffering, and it would have been wise to avoid contact with them if at all possible. For the most part Washo life seems to have gone on unchanged. The cycle of movement was unaltered by the presence of this handful of white men. The Washo observed and learned something of these new people, watching for whatever new opportunity they might provide but unwilling to give up their own established and successful patterns. The fragments of European society lived among the Indians, not with them, and the Indians managed to avoid the strangers.

The Gold Rush

In 1848, a workman employed by John Sutter to build a lumber mill on the American River discovered gold. Sutter, an amazing and politically astute man with visions of empire, tried to keep the find a secret but the word leaked out and California's gold rush began. In the same year, the United States and Mexico signed the Treaty of Guadalupe Hidalgo, ending the Mexican War and bringing California under the American flag. With the war ended, a battalion of men raised in Utah to fight in California, the famous Mormon Battalion, began their march back to Salt Lake City. They constructed a wagon road over the Carson Pass and marched through the Washo country. Within the year, parties of settlers, colonizers from the Mormon state of Deseret, were moving into the Carson Valley. They intended to establish farms and a permanent settlement. They cannot have been completely insensitive to the commercial possibilities of raising food and animals on a direct route to the gold fields. The center of the Mormon colony was later to become known as Genoa. It was there, in the summer of 1849, that an enterprising man named Beatie set up a trading post for the season. It was also in the summer of that year that travelers crossing the Sierra set up many camps on the shore of Lake Tahoe, the heart of Washo life. At the same time, a party of 150 horse-riding Indians is reported to have appeared at the lake. These must have been Paiutes, newly possessed of the horse, beginning to expand and flex their military muscles. From this point on, Washo and white history became merged. Although the two cultures were separate and the two societies distinct, the behavior of one henceforth would have effects on the other. The Indian and white populations of the Washo country began to adjust to and depend upon one another.

By 1851 the Genoa trading post was being operated year-round. A number of gold seekers chose to seek the more mundane fortunes of agriculture and settled in the Carson Valley and near Honey Lake. Two years later, the trading post and scattered farms of the Carson Valley were officially organized into a town and settlements formed in Washo Valley and Eagle Valley. Mail and passengers were moving across the Sierra drawn by mule teams which left Sacramento three times a week headed for Salt Lake City.

The temporary camps on the shores of Lake Tahoe had become permanent trading posts in the mid-1850s. By 1858, a telegraph line connected western Nevada with Sacramento and the outside world. There were at this time not more than a thousand foreigners living within the Washo country. They were scattered over the best and most productive areas of the Indian land. Familiar with the aggressive Indians of the east and the Great Plains, the settlers expected to be attacked. That they were not is due to Washo caution and perhaps to the basic Mormon attitude, often violated in practice, of friendliness and consideration toward Indians. In 1858 the Comstock Lode, in the area of what is now Virginia City, Nevada, was discovered. The slow changes brought about by piecemeal and small-scale settlement ended abruptly and the course of Washo history took another direction.

The Comstock Lode

Silver was discovered in 1858 in the mountains east of the Washo country. In the following year, 20,000 fortune seekers swarmed over the Sierra Nevada. Great mines bored into the hills. Theaters, saloons, opera houses, hotels, bawdy houses, and elaborate churches were built with amazing speed. The silver barons erected mansions, their furnishings from Europe. Miners from the east and from Wales came to work in the mines. The famous entertainers played in Virginia City and hundreds of disreputable characters came to hover on the fringes of the great fortunes.

Within two years 5000 acres of land were under cultivation on the east fork of the Carson River. Ten thousand head of cattle, horses, and hogs were grazing on the most productive gathering land in the Washo country. The famous western explorer Major J. Dodge was appointed agent to exercise authority over the Indians of the region, including the Washo. From 1848 to 1860, the environment was changed dramatically and the Washo were forced to make adjustments to this new situation.

The New Environment

The small number of early settlers did not seriously discomfit the Washo, but they did presage the conflicts to come later. Each of the major white activities—farming, ranching, mining—had an effect on the environment which had to be reflected in Washo behavior.

RANCHING   In many parts of the United States, Indian tribes quickly adopted the practice of animal husbandry. The Washo, on the other hand, still look on cattle with some suspicion and hostility, and sheep are viewed with contempt and hatred. From the point of view of the gatherer and the hunter, livestock are competitors. Cattle and horses graze in the best collecting grounds, stamping and spoiling what they do not eat. Their grazing reduces not only the plant food available for man but drives off game animals such as the deer and antelope. Sheep, cropping ground cover to the roots, are even more destructive. The hog roots up valuable tubers, his sharp hooves cutting and killing the grass. Had the Washo been able to take advantage of the livestock by killing grazing cattle and using their meat, perhaps their response would have been different. But the Anglo farmers of western Nevada did not let their precious few animals graze widely and untended as did the Spanish grandees of the west and southwest. The Washo soon learned that to kill a cow or steer was to invite retaliation by bands of men with firearms and little concern with Indian lives. Thus, whole areas of Washo country were rendered less productive by grazing and there was no compensating factor involved. Ranching was a complete loss to the Washo.

FARMING   Farming had both pluses and minuses in the Washo ledger. Certain productive lands were taken away from them and planted to wheat, barley, or vegetables. But wheat and barley are useful foods and their seeds were scattered outside the farmer's fields to enrich the natural grasses. The edges of fields became good gathering grounds for a new type of sunflower. No white farmer was as careful a gleaner as a Washo woman and the harvested fields themselves were sources of seeds. The farmers also irrigated, and along the ditches a heavy growth of willow and cattail sprang up, providing habitat for cottontail rabbits, doves, waterfowl, and an important source of basket material. While farming took certain gathering lands away from the Washo, it provided compensating alternatives which permitted the Washo to continue living very much as they always had and still reap an advantage.

MINING   Mining required large numbers of workers. The mining cities soon drove away the larger game. Mine tailings blotted out good picking grounds and created ugly barren hillocks. Most importantly, the silver industry demanded lumber for mine shorings and charcoal for smelting. The groves of piñon trees on the nearby hills provided both. Today the hills near Virginia City are nearly barren. Before the mines were sunk, both the Washo and the Paiute had picked pine nuts in this area. At first the white men cut the trees, but soon employed Indians to do the job and finally, because they could not depend on Indians, Chinese took over the task of cutting the trees and making charcoal. Washo prejudice against the Chinese is based on the fact that the orientals wiped out the sacred piñon groves. This may be a post-hoc rationalization and the real resentment may have arisen from the fact that the Chinese drove the Washo away from a profitable occupation. In general, mining was a total loss to the Washo hunting and gathering economy. On the other hand, it was in the mining towns that the Washo began to learn a most important lesson about dealing with the white men. The whites were willing to pay money for labor and if a man had enough money, he could buy any of the desirable things the white man brought into the Washo country.

Two Sides of the Mirror

The impression one group forms of another will play an important role in shaping the relations between the groups. The white impression of the Washo can be found in old records. The Washo impression of the whites is a more difficult matter to determine but well worth examining.

POOR, NAKED SAVAGES   Typical of early white response to the Washo is the following quotation:

They are more filthy than beasts and live in inhabitations which summer or winter are nothing more than circular enclosures, about five high without roof, made of artemisia or sagebrush, or branches of cedar thrown about the circumference of a circle and serve only to break the wind. (Ingalls 1913)

The same observer reporting on Washo clothing said:

Their dress, summer and winter, is a rabbit skin tunic or cape, which comes down to just below the knee, and seldom have they leggings or moccasins. Children at the breast are perfectly naked, and this at a time when overcoats were required by Captain Simpson's party. Women frequently appeared naked down to the waist and seemed unconscious of any immodesty in thus exposing themselves.

To men experienced with the Indians of the plains or the plateau, who were clothed in deer skin and wrapped in buffalo hides, riding horses and living in warm tipis, the Washo must have appeared to be inferior persons indeed. Moreover, a people so devoid of national pride as not to attack the whites, which many of the settlers fully expected, attracted the contempt of the invaders. And, as soon as it seemed clear that the Washo were not going to make any general resistance, their demands and welfare could be ignored. Many people saw the suffering of the Indians in the winter, knew of deaths from starvation and either consciously or unconsciously recognized their responsibility for having ruined Washo hunting and gathering grounds. It was more comfortable to consider these unfortunates as inferior humans without the intelligence or ambition to avoid their fate. The Washo were always seen as a very small tribe without power, subservient to the more threatening Paiutes. This impression stems in part from the fact that the Washo seldom assembled en masse. Settlers saw only individual families or, at the most, local bunches and thus never considered the Washo as a single people.

The Paiutes had, by the late 1850s, begun to form war bands and raid white ranches and wagon trains as well as Washo encampments wherever they were found. The Washo were in fact ground between the short-lived but violent militancy of the Paiute and the relentless expansion of the whites.

THE POWERFUL BEAST   The Washo view of the white man is as much a reflection of his ignorance as is the white view of him. All things in the Washo world had a power of their own. Into this world came the white man who possessed more power than the most powerful and fearsome foreign Indian. His guns killed from great distances. He tore up the earth with plows and sent huge holes plunging into the hills. He controlled fearsome beasts, cattle, oxen, and horses, and he was quite unpredictable. As unpredictable, in fact, as a bear driven out of his cave or a man with bear power. All of these things were *mushege* or "wild." But the white man was the most fearsome *mushege* of them all. This suggestion of Washo attitudes toward the whites is found in their word for white man, *mushege*, which is the same word used for fierce animals or bad-tempered men. Today the word carries a connotation of insult and implications of madness or insanity. But then, to the Washo, much of what has happened in the past century must seem mad indeed. The Washo did not resist the white man for a number of reasons, not the least of which would seem to be the fact that he considered his own powers as insufficient to the task.

The New Alternatives

The Washo, unlike the Paiute, found himself virtually overwhelmed by the newcomers. The Paiute raider could flee into the vastness of Nevada and escape. The Washo had no place to hide. On all sides there were towns, ranches, farms, trading posts, stage stations, and railroads. The high mountains could not provide a refuge during an entire year. The Washo chose to adjust to the new world. Old resources were gone or reduced but the white man provided many opportunities for those who would take advantage. And the traditional life of the Washo had shaped a people ready to seize whatever advantage that came to hand.

The greatest new resource was the white man himself. Few in number, bent on success and fortune, there was more work than he could do. Much of it was the dirty drudgery of civilization which he did not want to do. The Washo were willing, even eager to supply his needs. In the fall, the Washo had always settled in their camps and collected great piles of firewood against the winter cold. Farmers were willing to pay to clear greasewood and sagebrush from fields. The Washo made new winter camps near a farm and, after the pine nut harvest, after the fall deer hunting, after the rabbit drives, he could work for pay. Sacks of potatoes or wheat flour, a side of beef, hams, and bacon made winter food more certain than in the past. The traditional cycle had to be altered only slightly in order to adjust to a new resource. In addition to earning food or money the Washo found the habitation of the whites a treasure trove. The whites soon accumulated refuse piles and garbage heaps. What was waste to the newcomers was a bonanza to the Indians. The slaughtering of a steer or hog left entrails, heads, hooves, and tails, all edible in Washo eyes. Although the white man might be contemptuous, the Washo was too overwhelmed by his new riches to notice. The castoff clothes of the white town, tattered and worn, mended and remended before being discarded as hopeless, were still better than nothing. Moreover, wearing clothes gave them more freedom of movement. Naked Indians were offensive to the Victorian eyes of the mid-nineteenth century. A pair of tattered trousers or a stained and much patched dress permitted a Washo to enter the town.

The willingness to beg food, clothes, or money was another mark against the Washo in the eyes of the white men. If we view it through Washo eyes, it is an understandable consequence of the situation. It was never against Washo ethics and manners to ask for food. It might not always be given, but generosity was a virtue aspired to by all Washo. It was not demeaning to ask for what one desired, particularly when the one you asked had such an immense store of riches and never seemed to suffer from hunger and cold. It was demeaning to refuse to give what one could spare easily. When the settlers were few, begging had taken the form of demands which were often met. Sometimes these gifts were conceived of as rents for Washo land, or so it was interpreted by the whites. The Washo came to feel the payments were their due, although they made no attempt to enforce payment by resort to violence. Many settlers appeared to find it was easier to make a few presents as a bribe to prevent stealing or, perhaps, to ward off violence which always seemed imminent to the whites. Begging, then, was only an extension of a relationship which began to take shape almost with the first white-Indian contacts in the area.

Stealing was also a source of income for the Washo. As early as the 1850's, a band of Washo had made off with horses tied outside a meeting house in Washo Valley. A posse formed to pursue them, routed them from around a fire only a few miles away busily eating one of the animals. Such lack of concern for pursuit suggests that the Washo did not expect it. A brief clash between whites and Washo near Millford, Caliornia, was known as the "Potato War" because a band of Washo had harvested three acres of potatoes without the permission of the owner. What set of misunderstood promises and conflicting expectations caused this "raid" will never be clearly understood.

The value of the white settlements was not limited to extensions of the old patterns of Washo gathering and gift giving. Ready to seize upon any opportunity provided, the Washo saw other possibilities in the presence of the whites. In the winter of 1857, an Indian leader called Captain Jim organized an entertainment for the whites in the Carson Valley area. The settlers were to come to a special Indian dance and bring a gift of a sack of flour. The value of a sack of flour in western Nevada was $8.00. The whites came, made their gifts, saw a number of Indian dances and games and were given a gift in return of a single deerskin apiece. The value of a deerskin at that time was $1.00. On a profit and loss basis, the Washo were singularly successful, but more important was the fact that they had obtained an important addition to their winter food supply.

In the first years, the Washo were successful in preventing the whites from fishing in Lake Tahoe. Threats of violence and occasional fist fights or clubbings discouraged white fishermen. By 1859, however, a commercial fishery had been established on the southeastern shore. There were already too many whites for the Washo to risk a battle. In 1862, white fishermen were using long seine nets, and by 1880, as many as 70,000 pounds of trout were being shipped from the settlement known as Tahoe City to be marketed in Reno, Carson City, Virginia City, and the other settlements. The Washo still made the annual migration to the lake, but some traditional fishing practices were discouraged. Fish traps were particularly distasteful to the whites. In 1868 an angry settler shot and killed a Washo he found building a trap. Oldsters still chuckle with merriment as they tell of white men who were beaten and thrown into a lake or stream when they tried to interfere with night fishing. Equipped with lake-worthy boats copied from models used by the whites, using long lines and steel hooks, the Washo themselves took to commercial fishing. Taking what they needed for food, they sold the surplus at Tallac on the shores of Lake Tahoe or hawked fish in the streets of Carson City and Genoa. A gunny sack full of average-sized fish sold for somewhere between one and two dollars. However, a large fish of four or five pounds or more was taken immediately to the hotel at Tallac and chances were sold at twenty-five cents apiece, the winner taking the fish and the Washo realizing several dollars.

Commercial fishing was practiced all during the fishing season on every stream and lake in the area. Tensions between white and Indian fishermen came to a head in 1880 when an attempt to prevent all trapping and spearing of fish in the streams leading into Lake Tahoe was made. The angry Indians banded together, prepared to resist in number, and restrictions were relaxed. Commercial fishing came to an end with the introduction of fish and game laws. These, in theory, also applied to the Washo. But a game warden was simply another white man to the Indians and an intercine war between the wardens and the Washo continued on all the fish-bearing waters of the region. Washo were arrested and jailed. Wardens were beaten or made fools of, and the Washo continued to sell fish to the white residents of the area who took none too kindly to fish and game laws themselves. This game of hide and seek over fish and game has not entirely disappeared, and it is a rare year that some Washo is not arrested for violating one or another of the game laws of two states.

The enormous amounts of fish taken from Lake Tahoe by commercial fishing greatly reduced the supply of fish in the entire area drained by the lake. Increased pressure of white sport fishing further reduced the fish supply. Fish and game laws made it increasingly difficult to fish. Land along the shore of the lake became more and more thickly settled. Clashes between whites and Indian fishing parties became more frequent. Gradually, fishing in Lake Tahoe became less and less important to the Washo. Well into the twentieth century, some bands still migrated there in the spring, but the great spawning runs were no more. When the energy expended was greater than the return, the Washo gave up. Today an occasional Washo, with fishing license or without, may spend an afternoon at the lake or in some tributary stream fishing, but fishing has not been a major source of either food or monetary income for the Washo for at least three decades.

A few Washo men in their late fifties and sixties know how to use a pronged fish spear while standing waist deep in a mountain stream, but probably no fish have been taken by this method for twenty years. Today, the streams and lakes are stocked artificially to supply the enormous demand of sport fishing. White fishermen look on Indian spearing methods as an unfair advantage and are quick to complain. Some older Washo still carry a three-pronged fish-spear head in their autos or keep one in their houses. Inasmuch as the ownership of such devices is against the law, this constitutes a final defiance of the white man.

In summary, fishing has played an important role in the acculturation of the Washo. The Indians were quick to learn white techniques of fishing to increase their catch and turned to commercial fishing very early, thus involving themselves in the white economic system. In a time of reorganization of subsistence activities, fish continued to provide food but, more importantly, they provided money with which to buy food. Moreover, commercial fishing required capital investment in boats, fishing line, and steel hooks so that some Washo fishermen became entrepreneurs. Less certain is the role that defending their fishing rights against the whites played in creating tribal unity.

Hunting

Firearms and the competition of cattle and horses soon killed off or drove away the pronghorned antelope. Some of the oldest Washo remember stories told by aged relatives about hunts staged in their youth. This suggests that the old style antelope drive disappeared among the Washo perhaps as early as the 1860s. Men with power to dream of antelope and to charm them were, therefore, without opportunity to exercise their gifts. When they died, the entire complex of practice and ritual of antelope hunting came to an end. Those social bonds related to the antelope disappeared. Although the social consequences of the communal hunt were important, the relative rarity of the antelope in the area meant that it was not a major resource. The deer continued to be the main quarry of Washo hunters.

A man with a rifle or even a shotgun was able to kill deer from a much greater distance than was an archer. The old skills of disguise and imitation were no longer necessary. Older men continued to use the bow and arrow until the 1890s and, we can presume, continued to stalk game in the old manner. But their sons quickly abandoned the bow in favor of firearms. An additional factor was the presence of white hunters who might easily mistake an Indian in a deer-head disguise for a real animal.

The knowledge and skills of bow making disappeared along with the use of this weapon. By the turn of the century, some older men still knew how to make bows but younger men saw no reason to learn. Firearms made hunting a more certain occupation and may have reduced the felt need to insure success through ritual. Women were, and to a large degree still are, forbidden to handle rifles. Menstruating women in particular should avoid touching a gun. But on the other hand, hunting power became much less clearly defined in the Washo mind. The bones of deer were still treated with some respect, but each generation observes these rituals less rigorously than the last.

Hunting continued to play an important role in Washo economic life. The practice of burning the forest to drive out deer was soon discontinued, in part because of white objections. Driving deer into an ambush continued to be a popular hunting method. In that way, men who did not possess guns could obtain meat by serving as beaters. Game laws began to restrict the freedom of the Washo hunters. A severe decline in deer population east of the mountains meant that nearly every hunt required a long trip to California. The long trip, problems created by white trespass laws, protests from California Indians, alternate sources of income, and the practical Washo point of view which carefully weighed effort against return, all combined to limit the role of deer hunting. For the first time, Washo men might grow to manhood without developing the skills of a hunter, preferring to work for wages, sell fish, beg or scavenge instead of undertaking arduous trips to the west. But in some families, at least, boys were required to undergo their initiation test until the late 1930s.

Conservation laws worked to restore the deer population and many Washo men hunt regularly today. One or two deer are still to be found hanging in Washo homes in the fall. Theoretically, the Washo are required to purchase a hunting license in the state in which they hunt and to observe open seasons, bag and sex limits, and other game laws. Most Washo hunters stubbornly refuse to obey these laws which they see as infringements of their right to hunt in their own territory. Arguing that inasmuch as they have no reservation and have never received compensation for their lands, they have the right to hunt on "Indian Land" as do any other Indians living on a reservation. Indian lands, in their minds, encompass all that once was Washo hunting territory. Federal and state authorities do not agree with this interpretation. Every fall, Washo men are arrested for violation of the game laws relating to deer hunting. Deer meat often is the margin between eating and starvation even today, and the Washo feel they are unfairly treated. There are no exact figures on how much deer hunting still contributes to Washo subsistence, but in many families the lack of deer meat would be a serious hardship. More importantly, surrendering to white law would be a final denial of Washo heritage and subjugation to white society which has already taken so much from them.

With the decline of deer hunting, rabbit hunting became even more important. Tales of simply stripping the skins from rabbits and leaving the carcasses recall a time before the childhood of most elder Washo. In their childhood, every rabbit was eaten or dried to be stored against the winter. The hunting net disappeared by the early 1900s. When in the 1890's a net drive was staged at the Stewart Indian School, a net had to be borrowed from Paiutes living near Walker Lake. None was available among the Washo in Eagle and Carson Valleys. Instead, an arc of men armed with shotguns would move across the drive area, flushing the rabbits before them. Unlucky hunters or poor shots usually could count on being given some of the take of their more fortunate fellows. In the 1900s, when old men who still used the bow were alive and many middle-aged men still used muzzle-loading weapons, three different drives might be staged in the same area at the same time.

Rabbit hunting is one of the few examples wherein the adoption of the horse played any significant role in Washo life. A man collecting rabbits on his belt soon found walking difficult and steadying himself for a shot almost impossible with as many as seventeen swaying rabbits hung around his waist. Seventeen is invariably given as the top limit for a day's hunt unless a man had a horse. If he did, his son, nephew, or younger brother would follow the gunner and pack the rabbits on the horse. A good hunter could kill upwards of forty or fifty jack rabbits in a morning's shooting. Rabbit hunting was encouraged by white farmers and ranchers who considered the big hares a pest. This resulted in the increased importance of the rabbit boss. Men who dreamed of rabbits and called their neighbors together for a drive became more and more like minor "chiefs."

Claims to leadership in the tribe today are occasionally made because of descent from some particularly well-known rabbit boss. Rabbits are still hunted, but the old practices have all but disappeared. As food, they are not important enough to justify leaving wage work to hunt. Almost invariably, a hunt takes place on a week-end and seems as much sport as necessity. The rabbit bosses have disappeared. Modern Washo life is such that the random inspirations of a dreamer are transcended by the demands of a white employer. There are men who always seem to attend rabbit hunts and who seem to always take charge. They may pray quietly to themselves away from the rest of the hunters before the drive starts. Today, rabbits are usually fried and eaten when they are killed. Dried rabbit is scarcely considered palatable food by any but the oldest Washo. One man keeps two dried rabbits hanging in a shed near his home. They are more desiccated symbols of his Indianness than potential meals. Some day, one of his daughters, her hair in curlers and perhaps wearing high-heeled plastic shoes, will take the rabbits down and throw them away. He will grumble a little but it is doubtful that he will ever bother to dry another rabbit.

The shotgun made it possible to kill birds, both upland game and waterfowl, much more easily than any of the older methods. The preponderance of small game in the late nineteenth and early twentieth centuries made the shotgun more prized than the rifle among the Washo. However, the great numbers of wild fowl soon disappeared under the terrible hunting pressure of market hunters and sportsmen. Today, few Washo would invest the effort in either quail hunting or waterfowling. The prairie chickens and sage hens which used "to cover them hills like snow" have long since been killed off.

The presence of the white man created new opportunities for hunters, as it had for fishermen. Venison could be sold to restaurants and hotels, as could wild fowl of all kinds. Washo hunters became professional market hunters and contributed to the decline in game. The wildcat, a relatively insignificant species in aboriginal times, became an important source of income. The Chinese formed a large minority population in most western towns. They believed that the wildcat meat was a restorative of sexual vigor. Washo hunters sold all the wildcats they caught at high prices. Some men trailed the animals during the winter in the mountains along with the aid of dogs. The use of dogs for tracking may have been aboriginal but this is not at all certain. Certainly traveling into the snowbound mountains in order to hunt wildcats was a new idea. One which once again reflected in the individual Washo's ability to seize new opportunities when they appeared.

In aboriginal times, the killing of a bear was a dangerous and relatively infrequent event. The possession of a bearskin robe was the sign of a man possessed of courage and great power. Armed with a gun, any man was able to kill a bear in relative safety. Soon the possession of a bearskin robe was common among most Washo men. One old white settler, born in the Carson River country in the 1870s, reports that almost every Indian man who died was buried in a bearskin robe. The ability to obtain the symbols of courage and power which had once been the possession of only a few respected men may have encouraged many men to claim the status which the symbol once designated.

Gathering

The appearance of the white intruders and their livestock upset but did not entirely destroy the aboriginal pattern of gathering. There is evidence of hardship in the early years, but we cannot discount the possibility that the attractions of living near white towns led many Washo to abandon their traditional gathering rounds. In this case, starvation or near starvation can be blamed not on an absolute lack of resources as much as to a change in social and economic patterns. However, as early as 1861, a United States Indian agent reported that the Washo's condition was due to the activities of the whites. Already, many of the tribe were reduced to accepting federal rations. The very willingness of the federal government to feed Indians may have contributed to the Washo failure to collect enough food in the traditional manner, preferring to take advantage of the new resource rather than search out unspoiled areas.

The pine nut was not too seriously affected save around the mining towns. In other areas, the nuts were regularly gathered and stored against winter. The groups which were left without a source of pine nuts had to move into the gathering areas of others, thus putting a greater strain on the supply. However, in aboriginal times, it seems clear that far more was gathered than could be consumed, and Washo storing methods were so primitive that as much as half the supply was allowed to rot or be eaten by small animals. If the following year was a good gathering year, the stored surplus was simply forgotten. Thus the abundance of nuts served as a resource even in the most dismal period of Washo history. In general, the new situation created few changes in pine nut gathering methods. The same knocking sticks were made and the nuts struck down in the same manner. In the fall, after a *gumsaba,* the families repaired to their gathering grounds, marked with rocks to show the boundary lines, and gathered pine nuts for from three weeks to a month. In the face of all the overwhelming technology of the newcomers, the gunny sack seems to have been seized upon earliest and with the most enthusiasm for collecting, carrying, and measuring pine nuts. Even today, the basic Washo measure of quantity is the gunny sack. Perhaps the adoption of the gunny sack for purely utilitarian purposes allowed the Washo basket weavers to devote their energies to the production of finer baskets for display and for sale to white people as souvenirs. In the years following the appearance of the white men, virtuosity in basket weaving increased. Some Washo women became locally famous as basket weavers. They experimented in size and design, often taking months to weave a single large and perfect basket. By the early 1900s, some Washo women had become almost full-time specialists in weaving. White collectors or traders supported these artists, giving them food, clothing, and a little money against their basket production. Though any Washo woman could make baskets and of course some were better than others, aboriginal life had not permitted such a degree of specialization.

Although the Washo were slow to adopt the horse and wagon, the gradual introduction of this means of transportation enlarged their gathering horizons. Trips with a wagon could be taken well into California to gather acorns and a single family could collect a wagon load rather than a few back-packs full. The old routes into California often did not provide grazing for animals. New trails and new camp grounds had to be found with an eye to the needs of the team.

The railroads also affected Washo gathering habits. The Indians were quick to learn that the land along the new rights-of-way produced exceedingly heavy crops of pig weed and soon the late summer saw many Washo families camped along the railroad tracks to take advantage of this new situation. It was also an early railroad practice to provide free transportation for groups of Indians. This was a nineteenth century "public relations" gesture to insure cooperation of the Indian tribes along the right-of-way who often warned friendly railroaders of washouts, fallen trees, and other dangers. During the late nineteenth and early twentieth century, Indians camped near a railroad stop until enough were present for the agent to assign an empty railroad car to take them over the mountains to California. The Washo scattered into the hills to collect berries and then would wander the streets of Sacramento and other California towns selling the fresh fruit. When the crop was exhausted, the Indians would entrain once again for Nevada. The familiarity of the Washo with plant life and their willingness to work patiently in the collection of seeds suited them for the demands of early-day farming. Washo women were employed to pick weeds from farmer's fields. This tedious hand-work was usually payed for in food. Even today, weeding gardens in Minden and Gardnerville, Nevada, is a source of income for older Washo women. Harvesting potatoes was another task assigned to the Indians who received their pay in kind. White men in the area developed an elaborate and often curious folklore about the abilities of Indians. One such belief was that Indians, particularly the Washo, were more skillful in stacking hay than were white men. Whether there is any objective truth to this belief or not, for many decades harvest time was important to the Washo because of the wages to be earned in the hay fields.

In general, the white presence altered rather than destroyed Washo gathering resources. New plants appeared which were quickly incorporated into the Washo subsistence complex. New areas became productive and thus altered the patterns of movement. On the other hand, trespass laws and barbed wire sharply restricted the ability of the Washo to move freely. Agriculture provided many opportunities for gatherers to earn money or food. Thus, the Washo continued to gather but the pure aboriginal pattern of gathering could no longer support the entire population. Some families continued to follow the modified movement cycle, others became increasingly dependent on the new alternatives. However, as the white population in Nevada began to stabilize, the Washo either had to make over-all adjustments or disappear. The opportunistic Washo chose to make the adjustment. However, they were made in keeping with Washo tradition, piecemeal, family by family, often person by person. Some were able to maintain a modified form of the traditional life, others chose to live in houses and work in occupations provided by the new civilization.

Today, gathering is still very much a part of Washo life. Near every settlement, hidden under brush to keep it from the whites who might laugh, is a *lam,* regularly used to grind pine nuts and occasional acorns. If a wet summer produces a large crop of wild mustard or pig weed, many Washo will turn out to gather the seeds. The pine nut hills are still full of Washo in the fall. But a Washo family can no longer move through the country seizing whatever opportunity the floral life provides. Gathering today produces supplemental food or income or provides a touch of nostalgic Indian identity but it can no longer support a people. The plants have grown too few and the needs and demands of the people have changed to fit a new model of the good life.

Indian Culture and White Economics

The Washo were fortunate that the earliest permanent white residents of this country were traders. From them, the Indians quickly learned the utility of money and how money might be earned. The whites had a great many things which were desirable to the Washo. Clothing, guns, knives, hatchets, pots and pans, and gunny sacks. Many of these things retained their desirability in Washo eyes long after they had become useless to whites. Guns cost a great deal of money but money could be earned. Within a few years after the first white settlement, Washo men were making long trips on foot to Sacramento where they bought guns. The fact that the whites occupied almost all of Washo country, leaving the Indians no refuge area in which they could isolate themselves, is also important. The two cultures were almost forced to adjust and adapt to each other. This adjustment, gradual and piecemeal, not without conflict but never involving the drawing of clear-cut lines of hostility between the two peoples, was one which for many years was of benefit to both sides. The farmers of western Nevada needed the Indians to harvest the crops. Indians were also useful as general farm laborers. Moreover, Indian girls and women provided a sexual outlet for ranch hands, a distinct advantage to a rancher who otherwise might lose his crew to the carnal attractions of Virginia City. Also, the Washo soon learned that while the white community as a whole might be indifferent to the winter suffering in an Indian village a mile away from a town or hidden in some mountain cove, few white ranchers would let Indians starve if he knew them. Individual families and bunches began to develop close relationships with individual farmers. In the spring, the Indians drifted into the mountains to fish and hunt, but as the summer wore on, they came back into the valleys to gather what wild food was still available and to work in the harvests, hold a *gumsaba,* pick pine nuts, and then set up a winter camp near a ranch or farm. If their food ran short, they could depend on the farmer to contribute a few sacks of potatoes or flour or even a side of beef for their survival. During this period many Washo began to adopt the last names of their rancher benefactors. Because Indian girls often bore the children of early ranchers, the names were often deserved. These Indian-white relationships were the basis on which many Indian families recognized their kinship to a white family. The whites, more inhibited about the sexual adventures of their ancestors, are less willing to openly recognize the relationship. But nonetheless, there is a curious unspoken recognition even today between Indian and white decendants of the same pioneer forefathers.

The relationship between individual families and bunches and individual farms and ranches made a distinct change in Washo living patterns. The more remote Indian wintering places tended to be abandoned and distinct Indian communities began to form around individual ranches or on the outskirts of towns. Irrigation ditches provided a water source and the opportunity for winter hunting in the new willow groves. Each year, the same families tended to return to the vicinity of the same ranch and distinct "bunches" developed.

Particularly in the Lake Tahoe area, lumber camps sprang up. Some Washo men found employment in the woods. A few became teamsters hauling logs. Others became lumberjacks and yet others worked at odd jobs around the camps. The most important effect of lumbering, however, was that it provided a basis for Washo attempts to winter in the high mountains. The lumber companies left watchmen in the camps during the winter. These lonely men welcomed the company of any race. In the 1880s, some Washo families set up permanent camps near the lumbering operations. Old men who were boys during this period fondly recall the white watchmen cooking flapjacks in return for companionship in the snow-filled forests. As early as the 1880s, some Washo had become well enough versed in white law and customs to attempt to take advantage of the Homestead Laws and filed claims on desirable pieces of land. How many of these ambitious men ever succeeded in "proving up" and obtained full title is not known. As they were born and raised in a world with little or no concept of individal land ownership, their attempts are evidence of the Washo ability to adapt to new situations. Throughout the last quarter of the nineteenth century and until the end of World War I the Washo became increasingly involved in the economy of the white man. Several early-day newspapermen commented that the farming community of western Nevada could not operate without the assistance of the Indians. The importance of the Washo and their integration in a new social system is indicated by the fact that their activities were regularly reported by the newspapers of the day. The success of the pine nut harvest was reported as were Washo expeditions to catch wild horses in the pine nut hills. The deaths of prominent Indians were given attention. Accounts of their funerals were published in great detail. The tone of these stories was often patronizing, revealing a general attitude that the Indians were simple childlike people to be treated kindly if they behaved properly but to be punished severely if they transgressed. It was reported, for instance, how a marshal put a rope around an Indian man's neck and dragged him up and down the main street of Genoa until the Indian revealed where he had purchased a bottle of whiskey.

In the half century from 1850 until 1900, Washo life had undergone a number of gradual changes and by the latter date, a new balance had been achieved. No longer naked, the Washo had adopted clothing, and with clothing, they also became aware of shame. Nakedness was no longer acceptable even among the Indians. Washo innocence had been transformed into a prudishness equal to that of the whites from which it had been borrowed. Today, the single threat to the continuance of the girls' puberty ceremony is the modesty of the girls who object to being bathed in public even though they retain their underclothing.

The mountains still drew many Indians into the high country in the spring and gathering opportunities called them in the summer. The pine nut harvest was another occasion for moving, as was the opportunity to attend a girl's dance or some other gathering. However, the Indian towns around the white settlements became permanent. Individuals and families might leave and return but seldom were the towns abandoned.

Conflict, Cooperation, and Leadership

The change in Washo existence brought about changes in Washo social structure. The old institutions developed to exploit the aboriginal environment or to cope with foreign Indians were no longer functional. Indian wars were disruptive to white affairs and intertribal conflict was suppressed by federal troops. The Paiute Wars of the 1850s and 1860s ended in defeat for the Indians. For the Washo, this was a blessing. The new militancy of the Paiute had threatened Washo security and they were delighted to see the whites defeat and contain their old enemies. During the wars, many Washo served as guides and auxiliaries with white forces. Other bands divested themselves of their arms so they would not be confused with hostiles. The new situation made the "rough" Washo, the man who was careless of his safety and always ready to fight, a liability rather than an asset. Leaders of this type began to give way to men of a more conciliatory nature. When they had been more numerous than the whites, the Washo were willing to threaten violence to obtain concessions. As we have seen, when their vital interests were threatened, as they were at Lake Tahoe, the Washo were willing to fight or at least to bluff. But there never was a "Washo War" and conflicts which did develop were individual affairs. Hostilities of this nature were not infrequent. One band of Washo in Washo Valley north of Carson City were noted as horse theives and on several occasions a posse of angry whites was formed to punish the thieves. Other bands tended to ignore the event, certainly they felt no compunction to retaliate. Individual Washo, often drunk, attacked whites or attempted to obtain food by threats of violence. One young man in the 1880s caused a minor sensation by killing a number of dairy cattle and then fleeing into the mountains. Both the Washo and the whites with whom they fought over fishing seemed to view the hostilities as individual affairs to be settled man-to-man rather than by any collective action.

The Washo leaders during this period were for the most part peaceful men, manipulators, conciliators, very nearly confidence men, but seldom warriors.

In the early 1900s, a young man, Washo Jim, attempted a reconciliation with his wife who had left him to live with a white farmer. The young man, after first getting drunk, went to the farmer's house where he was met by his rival, beaten, and thrown off the property. The Washo all view the fact that he was beaten as inexcusable. His jealousy over the woman is not justification for a murder, or indeed even for disturbing the peace, however, they feel that a drunken man is not responsible for his actions. Washo Jim killed his wife's lover and fled into the Sierra. Posses and men of the law chased him, but he avoided capture. The local sheriff threatened to punish the entire Washo population unless the criminal was found. The surrender is illustrative of the intimate Indian-white relations of the region during this period. The murderer contacted a local white man and made arrangements to give himself up. The white man gave his personal assurance of fair treatment and trial, which he kept. The story of Washo Jim is still well known by all modern Washo, particularly in the area around Woodfords, California, and he is viewed as a kind of Indian Robin Hood.

Other Washo leaders are remembered as clever men who were useful in dealing with the whites. Unlike other tribes who often united behind a single man who acted as a link between the two peoples, the Washo developed many such leaders. In part, this was because the traditional Washo society was fragmented with many local leaders of limited influence. We cannot ignore the fact that Washo-white relations were themselves fragmented. Working on individual ranches, peddling berries, baskets, and other such activities brought the individual Washo in direct contact with the individual white. Knowledge of white ways and language was not the exclusive property of a single man who could use it to gain power among his own people. On the other hand, it was useful to the whites to deal with leaders who could, for instance, locate a law breaker. Out of these relations grew a uniquely Washo leadership type, which has come to be known as "the captain."

The Captains

It is difficult to determine the exact origin of the title captain among the Washo. Military rank was used as a form of address or title more freely in the nineteenth century than it is today. The leader of a wagon train or an Indian agent, was invariably called "major." Crew leaders on railroad and other construction projects were usually called captain, a fact testified to by the lyrics of many folk and work songs. It is probable that the Washo borrowed the term from railroad parlance. When employers needed workers, men of the law sought criminals, or if disputes sprang up, it was to the local captain that the white turned. There is little evidence that their power was any greater than that of the local leaders of earlier days. The Washo rallied around the man who could serve them the best. Some captains were felt to have supernatural power or to know prayers which were useful to the people. Others were simply wise men whose advice was frequently good. As in the past, the "jurisdiction" of the various captains appears to have overlapped and individual Washo could chose to follow a leader or not as their own interests seemed to dictate. Any working out of Washo "political history" is difficult because one of the earliest of these leaders chose the name Jim. This Captain Jim appears to have been quite successful in dealing with the white man and to have earned the respect of both peoples. His success led later ambitious men to adopt the name Jim. If such men were themselves successful leaders, their exploits were added to a growing legend of "Captain Jim." The first Captain Jim probably was already a leader at first contact. He negotiated with the whites for payment for a piece of land on which to build a stage station in Carson Valley. The Washo often speak of a "treaty" which they signed in the early days. No treaty was ever negotiated and the treaty of Washo memory may well be the agreement between Captain Jim and the stage company. Most certainly, it was this Captain Jim who traveled to Sacramento in 1851 to meet with the leaders of all the tribes of California and attempt to negotiate for payment for land seized by the whites. Such a treaty was negotiated and signed guaranteeing the Indians $1.25 an acre but it was never ratified by the Senate. The first Captain Jim's influence was confined largely to the southern portion of the Washo territory. His death in the year 1875 was reported in full by the local paper which referred to him as "King James I". A number of other captains led bunches of various size during this period and apparently contended for the role vacated by the first Captain Jim. Some of them are remembered today and their claims vigorously supported or, with equal vigor, denied by modern Washo.

By 1881, another leader named Jim had appeared, leading a band of about 375 Washo who lived in the northern part of Washo country. In the vicinity of Carson City, some 700 Washo looked to a man named Captain Joe for leadership and in the Genoa area Captain Dave was said to be the leader of nearly 2000 Washo. Two years later, a Captain Pete is reported to be the head of the Genoa Indians, suggesting how transient was power among the Indians. Typical of the confusion of names is the case of the second Captain Jim of the northern Washo. His Indian name was *Daokoye,* which means "big heels." This was mispronounced and he is sometimes referred to as Captain Hill and yet on other occasions as Washo Jim.

In the last years of the nineteenth century, another Captain Jim, whose Indian name was *Gumalanga,* appeared as leader of the Washo. Many modern Washo claim that his authority covered all of the Washo people. Others say he was only influential in the Carson Valley area. The last Jim appears to have been a man of supernatural power, a "prayer" as the modern Washo would say. He lived near Double Springs Flat south of Gardnerville, Nevada, and traveled little. He was devoted to the preservation of Washo identity and unity. He urged that the Washo give up white ways and return to the old practices. So completely had the Washo changed by the 1890s that the "old ways" were interpreted to mean wearing old cast-off white clothing rather than new clothes purchased in stores. It was he who announced the date and time of the *gumsaba* held during this period, and under his leadership these gatherings seem to have been more nearly tribal in nature than they were in the past. Many Washo claim that all the Washo gathered at Double Springs Flat, but it is doubtful that the northern Washo would travel all the way to the Carson Valley and then return to their own pine nut groves in the north. When older Washo describe the practices of the *gumsaba,* they usually refer to those held under the direction of the last Captain Jim. He is said to have been the last man to know all the prayers and songs. When he died, sometime in the early twentieth century, the annual *gumsaba* became more casual and informal. The leaders who stepped forward to replace him did not have his esoteric knowledge. An old woman who claims descent from this Captain Jim knows some of the proper songs and rituals of the *gumsaba* and has led attempts to revive the ceremony. The differences between the two Captains Jim are evidence of the changes which had taken place in the half century of white-Indian contact. The first great leader was an intermediary between Indian and white. The second man turned inward, emphasizing and attempting to preserve Washo separateness.

After the death of the last Captain Jim, no one appeared to take his place as even nominal leader of all the Washo. His daughter had married a man named Ed who assumed the title of Captain but his authority and influence were restricted to only a few families in the Carson Valley. Captain Ed's son Ed John has claimed to be chief of all the Washo since his father's death in the 1930s. His claim is ignored by all the other Washo save a few relatives and usually honored by them only when they are foced to live with him to share his old age pension checks. Ed John, now is in his eighties, volunteered to represent the Indians in a centennial celebration and was given a certificate naming him as chief of the Washo by the governor of Nevada. The certificate became the center of a three-sided comic opera episode as the Bureau of Indian Affairs and several other Washo claimants all contended with Ed John for the meaningless symbol of a nonexistent chiefdomship.

After the brief and partial unity under the last Captain Jim, Washo leadership became fragmented. Each band located near a white ranch seemed to produce its own captain and no single man was widely respected. In fact, the ancient position of rabbit boss, for a brief time, seemed to be more important than that of captain. Men who had the power to dream a rabbit hunt could, for this purpose at least, command the presence of Indians from throughout Carson Valley. Several modern Washo occasionally claim to be "chiefs" or captains because their father or grandfather was a rabbit boss. Today, a man who volunteers or is selected to carry out some group task, supervising the barbecue given by the sheriff, for instance, is called captain by those who help him.

Although from the point of view of the white man the Washo were dirty, underfed or eating refuse, dressed in rags, beset by idleness and strong drink, living in shacks or flimsy brush shelters, the Washo appear to recall the period around the turn of the century as sort of a golden age. Certainly all the ills seen by the whites existed and added to them were epidemics of smallpox, influenza, and measles. From the viewpoint of the Washo, they were in far better condition than in aboriginal times. Even ragged clothes are warm in the winter if one has ever experienced the snows with no clothes save a rabbit skin blanket. The garbage heaps of Genoa and Carson City contained many useful and palatable things. Their homes appeared flimsy, but, in fact, were probably more substantial than the *galesdangl* of aboriginal times. From the lumber mills they could obtain the slabs of bark taken from logs and of these construct a winter home far better than any they had built in the old days. A piece of discarded canvas thrown over some sagebrush was a better *gadu* than a windbreak using brush alone. As early as the 1890s, Indians around Woodfords had begun to build homes of board and bat construction. Although only a few families could support themselves entirely in the old manner, there were many new alternatives open to the Indians. It was during this period that we see an upswing of "big times," unassociated with the pine nut harvest or any other ritual occasion. As have so many other primitive people finding their way in a new world of surplus goods, the Washo devoted more time to leisure, to elaborate ceremonials or to recreational activity. In addition to the *gumsaba,* which became longer and more elaborate, local leaders began to hold gatherings called simply "big times" but carefully distinguished from the pine nut dances.

A Washo known as Doctor Bob who lived near Woodfords built a round, semisubterranean dance house after the manner of the California tribes and held dances and curing ceremonies. Gatherings devoted to gambling, dancing, and feasting were also held in the Woodfords area and are well remembered by many older Indians. A second dance house was built in the northern part of Washo territory. It is interesting that part of the change brought about by the white man was the borrowing of traits by the Washo from neighboring Indians, traits which had been known for a long time but which the Washo economy could not support in aboriginal times. Washo men, claiming to be chiefs or captains, adopted headdresses in the Great Plains style. These bonnets had been adopted by the Shoshone and Paiute during their short-lived attempt to develop a Plains style culture. The hand drum, absent in the aboriginal Washo culture, was borrowed as well as a number of gambling games and other traits. Gambling, always popular, became a major activity among the Washo. Newspapers often mention that the streets of the frontier towns were crowded with groups of Indians playing cards and Indian gambling games.

Perhaps the most significant evidence of the relative prosperity of the Washo in this period is the Washo response to the Ghost Dance and other nativistic movements among the Indians in the west.

Nativism

One of the expected responses of primitive peoples enduring the stress of rapid culture change is a turning to the supernatural world as a means of reducing the tensions which have no earthly solution. Usually such movements were initiated by a prophet, often a man who claimed to have died and returned to life or who had talked to God in a vision. The doctrine almost always included a rejection of many of the traits of white culture which had been borrowed. These nativistic movements occurred in the east among the Iroquois, sprang up in the Mississippi Valley in the early nineteenth century and reappeared in the west in the last half of the nineteenth century. Curiously enough, the two most famous movements called the Ghost Dances were initiated by men from the same family, both Paiutes from Nevada.

The first Ghost Dance was taken up by some Paiute groups but found its most eager converts among the dispossessed and dispirited tribes of California. The impact of the Gold Rush had all but destroyed the Indian cultures over much of that state. Indians were many times shot on sight. Posses, calling themselves militia, staged Indian "wars" which were simply sadistic massacres. To the embittered and bewildered Indians, the promise of the end of this terror was a last bright hope and the Ghost Dances swept throughout the state. When the promise was not fulfilled, the cult waned but some of the rituals continued to be used.

In the late 1880s, the grandson of the first Ghost Dance prophet "died" and returned to life. He told enraptured audiences of his journey to heaven and his discussion of Indian problems with God. His sacred instructions included a dance and some songs. If these were faithfully performed, promised the prophet Jack Wilson, the white man would go away, the game would return, and the Indians would once again reign over their own land. This time the response came from the east. The tribes of the Great Plains, defeated in the Indian Wars of the seventies and incarcerated on the reservations, heard of Jack Wilson's wonderful promise. Delegations went to Nevada to learn of his experience. The Ghost Shirt Dance, so called because Wilson promised the followers immunity from bullets if they wore a special sacred garment, reached a peak among the

Sioux in the Dakotas. A few Washo are reported to have joined the Paiute in the dances of 1890 but the earlier movement appears to have had no effect on the Washo. While the religious mania swept through the Basin and Plateau, over the Rockies and across the Great Plains, the Washo continued to work out their own destiny. There is a strong argument in this that the Washo did not view their situation as desperate or indeed, even uncomfortable. There are elements of nativism perhaps in the doctrine of Captain Jim but they appear to be more the advice of a wise old man to avoid excesses than the promise of an inspired prophet.

The Washo had experienced great changes in their lives since the white man first appeared. But the nature of these changes did not create the dislocations and disorganization so common in other tribes.

Tribe and Government

It is impossible to speak of the changes in Indian culture without discussing, however briefly, the role of the federal government and its policy toward Indians. In the earliest phases of white-Indian contact, the Washo country was so remote that there was some doubt as to jurisdiction. The political ambitions of the Mormon leader Brigham Young were to establish a theocratic hegemony over much of the intermontane and Great Basin region, independent of the United States or any other power. The first Mormon settlers in the Genoa area probably intended to expand the state of Deseret, as the Mormons called their territory. These ambitions were soon abandoned in the face of the power of the United States, and Utah became a territory which included the entire area of Nevada. Because of the importance of Nevada silver and the area's increasing population, a separate territory was established in 1861 and the state admitted to the Union in 1864. The boundary between California and Nevada bisected Washo territory, a fact which complicates Washo-federal relations even today.

The federal government has always assumed responsibility for dealing with Indian tribes. Until the 1870s, Indian tribes were considered to be separate and sovereign nations. In the east where the tribes were more sophisticated, this argument had some validity, but even there the treaties and agreements were more frequently broken than observed. In the west, where political structure was weak and often entirely lacking, the idea of Indian sovereignty led only to confusion, misunderstandings, half-understood promises being given and broken and treaties ignored until the legal fiction could no longer be maintained. During the administration of President Grant, the policy of treating Indian tribes as separate nations was abandoned and the Indians were ruled to be wards of the federal government. In 1859, Major James Dodge was appointed Indian agent for Nevada. He was responsible for dealing with all the Indians in the area, both Paiute and Washo. Dodge appears to have dealt principally with the first Captain Jim and the Washo in the Carson, Washo, and Eagle valleys and around Lake Tahoe. He did report two other bands, one under a man named

"Pos-Larke" and the other led by a Washo named Deer-Dick. Dodge recommended that a reservation be set aside for both the Washo and the Paiute but no action was taken on this suggestion. Dodge was struck by the suffering of the displaced Washo and wrote a poem inspired by the finding of two Washo who had died from starvation. (Price 1962)

> Many a weary day went by
> While, wretched and worn he begged for bread
> Tired of life, and lowing to lie
> Peacefully down with the silent dead,
> Hunger and cold, and scorn and pain
> Had wasted his form and seared his brain;
>
> At last on a bed of frozen ground,
> In the Sierra Nevada was the outcast found.
> No mourner lingered with tear or sighs,
> But the stars looked down with pitying eyes,
> And the chill winds passed with a wailing sound,
> O'er the foot of the mountain where the form was found,
> But where every human door
> Is closed to children accursed and poor
> Who opened the heavenly portals and wide
> Ah! God was near when the outcast died.

Neither official reports or flights of poetic inspiration moved the government and three years later Warren Wasson, a new Indian agent, made a report to the governor of the Nevada Territory, that some 500 Washo in his jurisdiction had requested assistance because much of their hunting, gathering, and fishing territory had been despoiled by mining and ranching. In 1887 the Daws Act authorized the government to make individual allotments of land set aside for Indians. The pine nut hills were set aside as tribal land and allotments made. The purpose of this division of allotments was to provide the Washo with land on which to live. However, there are few water sources in the pine nut hills and game was scarce. Moreover, the winters are severe and the Washo never wintered there. Unlike many other tribes, the Washo could not be induced to sell their allotments. The pine nut continued to be too important to Washo existence and the groves became more and more important as symbols of Washo identity as the ancient culture gave way under the pressure of the white presence.

In the 1890s, Captain Jim and another Washo leader, Dick Bender, were called to Washington to testify on the condition of the tribe. There is no exact record of what they said, but Washo imagination has it that the respected leader was given the privilege of the floor of the House. Accounts of his speech to Congress are examples of the oratorical imagination of the American Indian. Whatever really happened, little came of the trip. In 1917, a pioneer rancher donated forty acres to the Washo tribe. This land was held in trust for the

Washo and until the late 1930s constituted the only land actually owned by the Washo people as a whole. It is the site of the present "Sagetown" Washo community.

In the late nineteenth century, the government established an Indian School, operated by the Bureau of Indian Affairs at Stewart, Nevada. For years this school served the Washo and Paiute and played an important role in the adjustment of the Indians to white culture. Indians were taught trades and agricultural skills. The school was also headquarters for the Indian agent, responsible for the area. But even today, the scattered and mobile Washo continue to be an administrative problem. Exact numbers are lacking, many Washo have no contact with the agent: for the rest contact is infrequent. The situation is further complicated because of the Termination Act of 1953 which ended federal responsibility for all the tribes of California. Because these California Indians frequently live in Nevada for long periods, they move in and out of federal jurisdiction.

The Washo Tribe came into existence in 1937 after the passage of the Indian Reorganization Act of 1934 which authorized Indian tribes to elect their own governments and manage tribal affairs under the supervision of the Bureau of Indian Affairs. The Washo have not been very successful in the conduct of tribal government. In addition to the Sagetown plot, the tribe now owns 795 acres purchased by the government in 1938. After a few unsuccessful years of attempting tribal management, the lands were leased to white ranchers, the lease being supervised by the Indian agent at Stewart. Most of the pine nut area has also been leased to sheep grazers with the Bureau of Indian Affairs acting as agent in the arrangement. During the same period the government responded to the needs of the Indians in Nevada (and the demands of the whites who objected to the conditions of "Indian Towns" in the vicinity of white communities) and established a number of small communities or "colonies." As early as 1872 a reservation had been set aside to contain the warlike Paiute. Since that time no land had been set aside for the Nevada Indians. By the time redress was made there was no suitable large area available, so the colony system was begun as a compromise.

A detailed discussion of Washo-government relations would be out of place in this context. We can, however, see that the relation has always been tenuous and seldom has the government impinged on the individual Washo life. As compared with other tribes, many of whom experienced two generations of total control of every phase of life, the Washo were singularly free to work out their own destiny. This freedom has had both positive and negative consequences. Certainly the Washo are poorer for not having assigned to them a large tract of reservation land. Tribal unity certainly has suffered from having no common ground for all the Washo. On the other hand, the Washo have been free to make their own mistakes and to learn how to live in the modern world. Many individual Washo have been relatively successful in finding a place in American society. The condition of many Washo today is exceedingly poor, but it would be difficult to prove that this is due to the lack of government control and supervision. Nor can one argue that the successes of the Washo are due to government programs.

The End of the "Good Times"

Before World War I, the Washo had managed to make an adjustment to the changed situation brought about by the intrusion of the white man. Although their position was far from ideal, the Indians had become a part of the society of western Nevada and eastern California. Farms and many businesses owned by the whites depended on the Washo population in order to operate successfully. The general attitude, as reflected in newspaper and other accounts, was one of paternalism. Indian families and bands had developed dependence relationships with ranches. Indian towns were a source of casual labor and domestic help for white communities. Moreover, Indians were customers of the white storekeepers. Their needs and desires had forced the Indians to depend on manufactured goods which cost money. This is not to say that the Washo had completely integrated with white society. For the most part, they went to separate schools, if they went to school at all. The Washo still made regular trips to the pine nut hills for the fall gathering. Some families continued to make hunting and fishing trips into the mountains. In the winter most Washo lived in a *galesdangl* made of boards, canvas, and brush. When families went on gathering trips or traveled to work on farms, they lived in the crude *gadu*. The Washo did not vote, they could not openly buy liquor. Law enforcement was often informal and frequently brutal. Nonetheless, the two parts of Nevada society, white and Indian were dependent on each other. Were either to disappear, the life of the other would change drastically. Despite the hardships and the handicaps of the situation, the Washo remember this time with nostalgia. Under Captain Jim there was a degree of unity and independence as a people. Food shortages and starvation might occur but they were much less frequent. There was work available for those who wanted to work. The demands of agricultural work fitted neatly into the traditional cycle of Washo life, that is, it was short term and intense, permitting the mobility which was important to the Washo. However, the Washo had reached an adjustment with a style of life which itself was already passing from the scene. The style of agriculture began to change. The fields of wheat, potatoes, and truck crops grown on family farms began to disappear. In their places appeared herds of white-faced cattle. The sheep grazing industry, which had begun in the 1890s, became more and more important. The need for men to plough and harrow, to harvest field crops and stack hay and feed chickens began to decrease. The cattle and sheep industries required fewer workers and those with skills the Washo had not developed. The Washo had never completely adopted the horse. Although many families owned a wagon and team and riding horses were common, the Washo were notoriously unskilled horsemen. The job of cowboy which attracted so many western Indians was one which did not appeal to the Washo. A few Washo boys were given temporary riding jobs but none became full-time cowboys. The lonely job of sheep herding was never interesting to the Washo. Sheep ranchers preferred to import Basques from Spain. These men, used to the long periods of loneliness and familiar with sheep, formed a nucleus of a new ethnic group in the area.

As roads were improved, the string of little towns along the eastern slope of the Sierra began to lose population. Originally these settlements had been formed along the route of the stage lines, each one forming the center of a local area of farms and ranches. With the end of the stages and the improvement of roads, such local centers lost their function. The Indian towns associated with each town also disappeared and the population of the Indian settlements near the larger cities swelled. As the need for labor in agriculture decreased the local bands also moved into the cities. A few families attempted to establish homesteads in California. As the Indian became less important to the functioning of white society, the white became increasingly hostile to the Indian way of life. The Indian towns were an increasing source of friction as white complained of immorality, drunkenness, and threats to health. The decade of the 1920s was a dismal period in Washo history. Gradually the bands dispersed. The last mobile identifiable band dispersed and settled down in the late 1920s. Without opportunity to work, the Indians became increasingly poverty stricken and desperate, unable to support themselves in the way they had learned in the past three generations, and equally unable to return to the traditional practices.

9

The Sad New World

NEARLY NINETY YEARS had elapsed from the time of the first appearance of white trappers and explorers to the late 1920s. It had taken
all this time for the Washo finally to abandon the last vestige of
aboriginal life. As early as the 1850s some Washo were taking advantage of
new alternatives presented by white culture. The old patterns of social organization had changed to fit new situations. The role of the antelope shaman disappeared, but the idea of a man with a special power involving communal hunting
continued to be expressed in the person of the rabbit boss. Gradually, a more
inclusive leadership developed under Captain Jim. Despite the fact that a few
people were still attempting to survive in a more or less aboriginal manner, the
first two decades of the twentieth century had seen the new balance achieved as
the Washo became more and more a part of the economy of the region. This is
a period of many "captains" and "chiefs." Each claimed recognition as the leader of all the Washo, although in fact their authority was local and sometimes
limited to a few relatives. The old skills of the hunter and gatherer were replaced or supplemented by those of a suppressed caste engaged in the hard
manual labor and low paying activities of an agricultural community. White law
enforcement officers and officials were increasingly important to the Washo
while native leaders lost their importance. Only one traditional role remained
essentially unchanged, that of the shaman. These men still carried out curing
rites among their fellows and were respected and feared because of the power
they controlled. In the absence of secular leaders, the shaman became increasingly influential. Seldom did they exercise direct power over a particular bunch or
band. Instead, they formed a distinct social type possessed of a kind of free-
floating political power, undirected because there appeared to be no place for it
to be applied. The Washo met the decade of the 1930s without formal leadership, without a distinct tribal structure, and with their place in Nevada society
rapidly disappearing. The unsightly Indian towns on the outskirts of Reno, Car-

158090

son City, Gardnerville, Minden, and other Nevada towns became increasingly irritating to the residents of these cities. In response to the demands to eliminate these communities the colony system was developed. Others moved into colonies near to (but not too near) Carson City and Reno. Permanent clusters of houses sprang up in the country near Woodfords and Markleville, California. Other families drifted west into California to live in isolation or join communities of other Indian tribes. The Washo genius for adapting and adjusting, for seizing new opportunities seemed exhausted. To add to the problem, the need for leaders was perhaps more acute than it had been since the beginning of the century. The isolation of the Indian population in colonies away from white communities created a more centralized Washo population. No longer could each Washo family go its own way, working out its own relationships with individual white men. The Washo had in some ways, become a "people." Because of their personal isolation, the Indians had become stereotyped. The conditions of the Washo communities were well known but the individual suffering which went with these conditions went unnoticed. Once again at least some Washo began to live in an almost entirely Washo world. The white world in which he had formerly moved, segregated and discriminated against, to be sure, but nonetheless a part of what went on around him, was now remote. The Indian town and the white town or city were now distinct places, one governed by city councilmen and protected by municipal or county law enforcement officers, the other vaguely controlled by the federal government. Socially, there was once again a field in which leaders might develop. Ideologically, there seemed no general agreement on what constituted a leader. The old patterns and beliefs which had joined the fragmented mobile groups of Washo speakers into a single people were no longer shared by all the people.

Some Washo had managed to avoid the economic deprivation experienced by most of the tribe. One of these was Tom George, one of three brothers who lived in the Woodfords area of California. Tom's father had been sometimes called the leader of the Washo after the death of Captain Jim, but this was disputed by most of the Washo. Chief or not, the elder George had been an ambitious and imaginative man who had begun to work as a guide for hunting parties and managed a mule pack train in the Lake Tahoe country as early as 1910. His eldest son Tom had taken over his father's business and continued to maintain the family fortunes as well as the respect of the white community earned by his father. Throughout the Washo country there were others like Tom George, men who had learned a trade or who had gone into business, one of them eventually becoming the owner of a saw mill and lumber business. Not a few of these men drifted away from their people, finding a place for themselves in the larger world. Some continued to think of themselves as Washo, although they publicly rejected many of the old practices of Washo culture which were so restrictive in the white world. Other families were able to maintain jobs working for white men and still live in Indian communities. The majority of Washo however, lacking education, their laboring skills less and less in demand, their English inadequate to life outside western Nevada, maintained a precarious existence in their colonies. The various claimants to captaincies or chiefdomships contended with each other, each with his own small group of supporters. The well-off frequently had no traditional basis for claiming leadership and the descendants of old-time leaders had no economic power. Nor was there agreement as to what aspect of power in the past constituted a valid claim to leadership in the present. Even those who did not claim to be leaders used their relationship to past leaders as a reason for not accepting the authority of some other person. Without reason for accepting the authority of one man whose advice was useful in meeting a specific situation, kinship and descent served only as a rationalization for claims to power. The only people who had real power were those who it was believed could cure illness or do harm to others. The shaman continued to perform curing rights, often for fees ranging from $20 to $60. But Washo life appears to have changed so dramatically that shamanism did not seem to be a means of finding security for the young men. The long period of training, the dangerous association with spirits, and the demands of one's power were restrictions that outweighed any benefits one might gain from becoming a shaman. Only a few young men attempted to learn the trade. At the same time, the fear of sorcery and witchcraft increased. With the old lines of society blurred and confused, everyone's hand seemed turned against everyone else. Accusations of witchcraft and campaigns of innuendo concerning certain people considered to be witches were common in every Washo community. The same beliefs in spiritual power which had shaped Washo aboriginal life now tended to disrupt it and create internal dissension. One reason for this may be the ending of the wandering way of life. The creation of increasing permanent settlements forced the Washo to live together in a way they had never experienced before. In the past, the hunting and gathering round and the cycle of agricultural work forced the Washo to move from time to time, meeting with other Washo, living with them for a time and then separating to move to some other area. In settlements like Sagetown, the tensions of communal living continued to build up, unbroken by the life of continual movement. It is probable that these tensions created the fears, anxieties, and hostilities which were expressed in terms of witchcraft accusations. Into this dismal situation two new factors intruded, a white man's law and an Indian religion.

The Legal Tribe

When Franklin D. Roosevelt was elected president in 1932, he appointed John Collier as Commissioner of Indian Affairs. Collier developed and saw the Indian Reorganization Act of 1934 passed into law. Indian tribes were authorized to elect councils, write constitutions, and begin to take over the business of governing themselves. The Washo took advantage of the law and set up a legal tribal government. This was the first time that anyone could speak of a political institution in which all the Washo, in theory at least, could participate and which could speak for all the Washo. Unfortunately, the Washo were unprepared for self-government as a separate people. A tribal council was elected and the form of self-government introduced. But the substance of self-government eluded the Washo people. Men who claimed to be chiefs continued to maintain their claims. The refused to accept the authority of the tribal council. Accusations of illegal acts and oblique accusations of witchcraft were made against council members and hurled back and forth between councilmen. Situations like this were common on many Indian reservations during the 1930s. Traditionally, Indian political ideology had not included the idea of majority rule. Indian groups preferred to delay decisions until persuasion, social pressure or exhaustion wore down the dissenter and resulted in unanimous decisions. American law, of course, has no real place for this kind of resolution. Therefore, Indian groups were forced to continue to operate within the new framework until they learned the methods of this new way of government. After nearly three decades of experience and education, many of them are becoming remarkably successful. For the Washo, the experience has not been sufficient. Without a reservation which would draw all the people together, forcing them, as it were, to learn a new way, the tribal form of government has had no real base from which it could operate.

Peyote, the New Way

As we have seen, Washo religion was centered around the concept of a personal experience with the supernatural, often in the form of a vision. This the Washo had in common with many other native religions in America. For the Washo the vision came unsought and unaided but among many other peoples the vision was actively pursued through fasting, self-torture, or the ingestion of hallucegenic substances; jimson weed, mushrooms, "red-bean," and the button of a small low-growing cactus known as peyote. Peyote was used in Mexico before the arrival of the Spanish. It appears to have been used aboriginally by some of the tribes in the southwestern part of the United States as well. In the 1880s a new cult based on the ritual ingestion of peyote developed in the Great Plains country and Oklahoma and began to spread in all directions among the reservation-bound Indians of the United States.

Some Washo may have known of the cult in the 1920s, but it was not until 1932 that peyotism found its way into the Washo country by a Ute shaman named Lone Bear. Lone Bear made a few Washo converts and held some curing meetings, but he was a notorious drunkard, often in trouble with the law, and the Washo avoided his peyote meetings.

Six years later, Franklin York, a half-breed Washo and a sometime bootlegger who had traveled widely over the United States in medicine shows returned to his home country to preach the peyote doctrine.

York was successful in spreading the peyote cult among the Washo and the neighboring Paiute. Soon his meetings were well attended and collections were often as high as $50. His first convert was a Washo shaman who combined traditional beliefs with peyote ceremonialism. Many of his other followers were the more acculturated and successful, people with steady jobs or even with businesses and bank accounts who had in large part abandoned their traditional past and, as the Washo put it, "gone the white man's way."

Very soon a schism developed between the more traditional peyotists and the more acculturated, some of whom were members of the tribal council. Before the dispute was over the matter had to be settled in a special hearing at the Stewart Indian reservation where accusations of marijuana use, witchcraft, and sexual orgies were made by the contending groups. Many of the Washo, in and out of the peyote movement, resented the fact that an Indian dispute had been taken to white authorities. Others feared the power of peyote as they had always feared supernatural power, pointing out that death, incest, and insanity were the consequences of partaking of the cactus. On the other hand, many others became devoted converts of the cult, traveling great distances to attend meetings and spending large sums to make the colorful feathered fans and beaded rattles which were part of peyote paraphanalia. Both traditional shamans and acculturated Washo, seeking a new basis for their claims to leadership of the tribe, experimented with the cult. Gradually, the old shamans died and none replaced them. Men who in the past would have become shamans became involved in the peyote cult seeking to become "chiefs," that is, people powerful enough to conduct meetings.

The peyote cult is a synthesis of native Indian beliefs and practices, incorporating the vision, drumming, singing, smoking, using the rattle, and Christianity. As such, it has a great appeal to Indians of all degrees of acculturation. Moreover, the benefits of peyote are open to all. Anyone may attend a meeting and eat the cactus and receive a vision. The dangers of power are not conceived of as being so great as were the dangers of power under the aboriginal system. They peyote cult takes many forms in various tribes, but the main outlines are the same wherever it is encountered. One of its primary commandments is a rejection of alcohol. Although there are many backsliders among the peyotists, the cult does give support to moderation in a facet of Indian life which was not present in aboriginal times when alcohol was unknown.

Peyote came into Washo life against the opposition of many whites. Although the cactus is not classed as a narcotic by the federal government, the Bureau of Indian Affairs was very much opposed to the cult. Perhaps because the cult gave Indians some organizational focus for their lives and made them more difficult to manage, perhaps because there was still a strong carryover in the Bureau from the days when Indians affairs were managed almost entirely by men appointed by the churches.

In the state of California the cactus was declared to be illegal, a law which is presently being challenged in the courts, and frequently county welfare agencies in Nevada refused to assist members of the cult. Some older Washo, grown used to the dependent relationship between Indian and white society, opposed the cult because it offended the missionaries who would then refuse to give Christmas presents and the like to the Indians.

In a sense peyote gave the Washo a sense of identity. In defying the white law and white disapproval and conducting peyote services, they were asserting themselves as Indians. Because peyote meetings were intertribal they were conducted in English and gave the Washo a sense of identity with other Indians. Most important was the fact that aboriginal religious practices, as meager and informal as they were, tended to disappear almost completely. The shaman no longer held sway in Washo life. The family rituals and ceremonials continued in many cases but almost as social conventions. Washo religious energy was devoted to the peyote cult. Even people who did not attend meetings became believers and peyote became the most powerful figure in Washo supernatural world.

The progress of the cult was not smooth. From time to time meetings would almost cease and only a few devoted adherents would remain. Then, inexplicably a new burst of enthusiasm would swell the meetings.

Today, because the Washo peyote meetings are the nearest ones to the urban centers of the San Francisco Bay area, the Washo country has become a center of peyote activity for Indians of many tribes. Indians living in the cities regularly make week-end trips to the Washo country to attend meetings. There they appear to renew their Indian self-image which enables them to return to the city and adjust to urban life for a time before they once again seek renewal.

To the Washo the changeover from the aboriginal religion to peyote is viewed as simply the addition of a new element of supernatural power provided to assist the Indian. The old patterns were not effective or needed in the new world. As one informant put it; "Them old doctors had to have a lot of power because the Indians didn't have (know) too much. But nowadays the white doctors have a lot of power and the Indian doesn't need his power anymore. But the peyote helps the white doctor take care of the Indians." It must be disheartening for the doctor in a modern hospital to realize that in the eyes of his Washo patients he is nothing more than a new and more powerful shaman assisted by peyote.

Sagetown

South of Gardnerville, off the highway and quite hidden from the traveler, is Sagetown. The forty acres of Sagetown sit dry and inhospitably on a bluff overlooking the Carson River. The road is paved part of the way to Sagetown, but until 1960 the road was unpaved and dusty and until 1941 there was no electricity. Even today, there is no sewage system and a single pump serves the entire population with water. The approach to the settlement is strewn with empty cans and wine bottles twinkling in the sun. Then a tangle of ruined automobiles purchased cheaply and abandoned when they quit running, stripped of spare parts to keep other cars running, appears. The houses are aged, unpainted board and batten structures. Between them is the litter of living: cans, bottles, old auto seats, and worn-out tires. And there are people. A young woman insensibly drunk; her child beside her on a cradleboard. An old man sleeping in the shade of a wrecked car, having abandoned his drunken trek home in favor of sleep. They both will wake sick on the cheap liquor and probably ashamed for having behaved like a "drunken Indian." They might even think about joining the peyotists in order to fight the temptation of the cheap barrooms of Gardnerville. From a ruin of a house a girl in her twenties emerges. "Hey white man," she shouts, "get this God damn white man outta my house." She is drunk and stumbles. From the house a white man, bleary eyed and unshaven, wearing dirty trousers and an undershirt, emerges. He curses the woman and she returns his obscenities with her own. They exchange ineffective blows and stagger together into the house shrieking with laughter. When she bears a child of this union she will probably not remember the man. The infant will be cared for by her mother and perhaps receive county welfare payments. Sagetown is sordid and if one sees no more than the surface of the community, fills the observer with hopelessness. Yet in the midst of Sagetown there are houses that are kept neat by Washo standards. Scrubbed children go off to the integrated schools of the white community. Young husbands and fathers go to work regularly, and their wives hang out wash and fight the relentless dust which sifts into the unsound houses. An old man spends his days painstakingly sewing beads onto baskets made by his wife in order to sell them to a tourist trading post. A middle-aged man and his wife walk along a nearby irrigation ditch selecting the best willow for basket weaving. She is an expert and her baskets sell to tourists in the California lake country. Sagetown is situated on the only ground actually owned and controlled by the Washo tribe. Its existence is an echo of a time long gone when the Washo were part of a social system including both whites and Indians. Although the Indians were viewed as inferior beings and certainly did not participate fully in white life, they were important to the economy of the area and the farmers and ranchers for whom they worked assumed some responsibility for the welfare of the Indians. Sagetown was given to the tribe by one such rancher for as long as the Washo continued to use it. Farm technology no longer needs a large local labor force to plant and weed and harvest. The Washo way of life, like that of many other minority peoples in the United States, is afflicted by marginality, a symptom of social and economic dislocation.

Economics

It is no longer possible to speak of a separate system of subsistence activities among the Washo. With very few exceptions, the economic alternatives open to the Washo are those open to any American. Wage labor is the only certain source of economic security. For most Washo this means work in the lowest levels of American economy. A few manage their own businesses. One operated a lumber company for many years and another continues to rent horses and operate a pack train for tourists. We have seen how changing agriculture virtually erased the special place the Washo held in the economy of the area. Today, Washo men compete with transient workers of all races for the agricultural work available. Some Washo are fortunate to have relatively regular but low paying jobs as gardeners in nearby white towns. Except for the few who have regular employment, wages usually are earned in seasonal activities. Construction work reaches a peak in the summer and Washo men, sometimes with their families, often without, scatter throughout the west to work where they can. Some few Washo, particularly the older people, manage to earn at least a few dollars by weaving and selling baskets to tourists.

A very few Washo have experimented with agriculture even as a subsistence activity. A very few today raise corn and a few vegetables for the table. The only attempt to farm commercially is being made by a young man near Woodfords, California. He grazes a few head of cattle on his allotment near the Carson River. In the fall, he helps his neighbors gather a winter wood supply and in exchange is permitted to cut the native grasses on their allotments and make a small hay crop. The only "native" activity which produces regular and important income for the Washo is gathering pine nuts. Many families go into pine nut groves and collect nuts, using very much the same methods as their ancestors used. Some of these nuts are kept as a part of the winter food supply. Some families sell the nuts locally, receiving from fifty to seventy-five cents a pound. However, nut gathering is hard work and the harvests are often uncertain. Measured in hourly earnings, the income is not great.

For many of the Washo, various types of pension and welfare payments constitute the only income. At times during the year, the only income in Sagetown consists of old age pensions, state and county welfare payments, and so on. In many cases, the only financial security afforded a Washo family is an elderly grandmother or grandfather who receives old age benefits. Many Washo have moved into California to live on family allotments in that state because the old age pensions are more liberal. Unlike many other Indian tribes, the Washo have no reservation which could provide a basis for economic development. In many cases, other tribes are involved in industrial activities, developing tourism, or exploiting the mineral, gas, oil, or timber resources. The Washo did not have these opportunities to develop their economic future on their own lands. Their future is linked inextricably with the society in which they live. For better or worse, the Washo are assimilated to American society albeit, for most of them, on the lowest and least profitable level.

Individuals have escaped the cycle of poverty completely. One such is a colonel in the United States Air Force, another holds an important and responsible position in the Bureau of Indian Affairs.

Residence

In the past, the cycle of subsistence determined the pattern of residence of the Washo. Gradually, residence patterns altered in order to take advantage of the new resources provided by white farms, ranches, and towns. Today, the Washo tend to cluster in settlements such as Sagetown or the various colonies in Nevada. Throughout the mountains on the eastern slope of the Sierra Nevada, individual families or small groups live on allotment properties in small communities. During the summer, many of the cabins and houses are abandoned as the family travels in search of work. The Washo are still extremely mobile and often travel to other Indian communities to visit relatives or attend ceremonies. Frequently, a family without income will spend weeks or even months sharing a cabin with some more fortunate relatives. Although the resources may be strained, this hospitality is seldom refused. When traveling, the Washo often camp, sometimes for weeks, wherever they find unoccupied lands. In the past few years, a few families have moved into permanent homes in the pine nut hills. The automobile, paved roads, and electric power lines into the area have made the region more habitable than in the past.

Society

The Washo are a society in the sense that they do constitute a distinct group of people with common heritage who interact with each other more than with any other group. However, there is little structure to Washo society. The old subsistence pattern has disappeared and with it the basis for the large units of Washo society. The old sectional "moieties" are vaguely remembered and some people still remember what group they were born into but the sections have little meaning. The bands based on antelope or rabbit hunting have all disappeared as have those which developed in relation to white farms or towns. Each Washo is in one sense at sea and on his own in a welter of individual social relationships which are without regular structure. The peyote cult may in the future provide a basis for new leadership and new social units. As yet, this has not completely developed. The legal basis of the tribe with the tribal council has not served to stabilize or reorganize Washo tribal structure. It seems unlikely that any future developments will lead to a self-contained tribal society for the Washo. Without a land base, there is little foundation for a tribal political system. Moreover, many of the functions of a tribal society have long since been taken over by white society, forcing the assimilation which exists today. White law enforcement and white laws govern Washo behavior. White government supervises the economic responsibilities carried out by the tribe in other situations. Welfare, charity, and old age security are functions of white government and it is doubtful that any Washo political body will ever have the vitality to take over these activities. In fact, the Washo are gradually becoming aware of their role in relationship to white society and government. In some areas, they constitute an important voting bloc and their favor is courted by local candidates.

The family still remains an essential and distinctly Washo social entity. The patterns of income have tended to develop a special family type based on the mother. The frequent absences of men working or looking for work and the fragile marriages which appear to be a result of the precarious economic situation tend to place the responsibility for raising children on the women of the family. Despite the pressures created by poverty, the Washo family today often follows a pattern not unlike the aboriginal family, that is, a married couple forming a core around which a number of lateral relatives and their children collect to live cooperatively. No longer is food gathered and shared but money is shared. Whichever member of the group works or receives a pension serves as the economic mainstay of the group.

Ceremonies and Recreation

The changes in economics and social structure have operated to erase from Washo life the ceremonial and recreational life which once set them apart. The *gumsaba* gradually disappeared in the 1920s and 1930s. An attempt to revive the gathering in 1953 was a failure. Only one person remembered the prayers and ritual, and she imperfectly. Moreover, she was feared as a witch. Only the older people attempted to recapitulate the traditional activities. The younger generations set up a phonograph in an empty house and held a white style dance. Neither group was happy. Oldsters say that in the event of poor pine nut harvests, the ceremony might be reinstated, but when the last people who know the ritual die there is little hope for the ceremony.

Shamanistic ceremonies have all but disappeared. One shaman is still alive but he has altered his ceremonies to conform to modern conditions. His curing sessions take only an hour or two. When he dies, another specialist in ceremony will disappear and the continunity of these skills will be impossible. Within the family the ceremonies, particularly those which did not require a specialist, persist in attenuated form. Women usually avoid eating meat for a time after they bear a child and sometimes observe the rituals related to bathing, hair cutting and the distribution of presents. As late as the 1930s, some young men went through the ritual of crawling through the antlers of a deer when they made their first kill. Some women avoid eating meat when they are menstruating if it was killed by someone they know. If the meat was purchased in a store, they do not observe the taboo.

The girl's dance is still held for every Washo girl when she first menstruates. Young girls today suffer some embarrassment in white schools, because the preparations and some of the taboos she must observe reveal her condition to her schoolmates, and insist on being bathed wearing a slip or brassier and panties. Perhaps the girls now in white schools will prefer their daughters to have puberty observances more in keeping with white style, but the ceremony seems still to have a great deal of vitality.

The games of field hockey, long distances races, archery contests, and the like which were important parts of any Washo gathering are no longer played. School-age children prefer basketball and baseball and dancing. Gambling in the Indian manner, which was part of every gathering, has also disappeared. People still play cards, but the motion pictures and gambling in the legal casinos serve as primary sources of recreation today.

The aboriginal ceremony related to death and burial was never complex. The casual and perhaps not universal annual mourning ceremonies have not been held for many years. White laws have forced the Washo to bury their dead in regular cemeteries. One such is a desolate and isolated patch of desert hillside known as the "Indian" cemetery. Another is a relatively well-tended plot near the Indian Agency headquarters at Stewart. Funerals are usually conducted by a white missionary. After the ceremony, however, an older Washo usually makes a short speech directed to the deceased asking him to leave the world and not bother the living. Frequently, the coffin is packed with the personal belongings of the dead. Larger belongings are taken into the mountains and thrown away or burned. Not infrequently a sick person is placed in a smaller shack, sometimes even a native style brush house outside the permanent home. This allows the deceased's family to burn down the secondary house without leaving the family without a home.

Food and Material Culture

A distinct Washo material culture no longer exists. A few people make rabbit skin blankets and nearly every family in the Carson Valley, at least, possesses one. Even these show the effects of change, with the strands being tied with cloth or string instead of sinew.

Basketry, the truly Washo art, is declining. Some few are made for gathering pine nuts and other baskets are woven for sale to tourists. Baskets are kept as nostalgic souvenirs of the past and one at least is found in every home. Near every Washo community a bedrock mortar or *lam* can be found. In many homes a *demge* is still kept. In the pine nut camps one can still see knocking poles, albeit bound with bailing wire, but still in the old tradition.

The Two Worlds

While the outward signs of Washo culture have disappeared and the Washo live in the world as it is, they have not abandoned their identity. The other world of the Washo is a world of the mind. The old tales are not forgotten, although they may be somewhat garbled and only half understood. The belief in the nature of power in the universe is still very real although its expression is most frequently found today in the peyote cult. Fear of the dead and concern about witches still sets the Washo apart from their neighbors. The patterns of leadership still rest on traditional attitudes toward human ability which are quite different from those of the white. Primarily, Washo identity is maintained by reference to the past. The features of the land on which they live have a different meaning to the Washo. Stories of old adventures, ancient miracles, and battles long past are told and retold and their locations pointed out. Stubbornly, the Washo view the land as being theirs. This relationship to the past was made real by the Washo claim against the federal government for the lands usurped without payment. The claim for 42 million dollars is before the courts and the possibility of a favorable decision helps provide a vague but real unity among the Washo people that is based on their past. This attachment to the land influences a retention of an attenuated version of the aboriginal annual cycle. In the spring and early summer, many Washo families travel to Lake Tahoe and the mountain lakes in the higher country. There they picnic and enjoy the scenery, the old members of the family telling traditional tales of the country around them. In a similar fashion, many families go into the pine nut hills in the fall, often for a single day, to picnic and gather a few pounds of nuts. These will be saved and eaten raw or cooked into the Washo favorite, a pine nut soup to be consumed in a single nostalgic meal. During the season, families will fish on some favorite stream and young men will go deer hunting. In short, the Washo has not changed his essential values in the face of a century of dramatic change. He has instead made whatever adjustments necessary to survive in a changing situation. The physical, economic, and social changes have been almost complete. The mental and ideological changes have been less extreme and constitute the core of Washo existence today. The conflict between the attitudes and ideologies and the realities of existence in the modern world is the basis of the Washo dilemma. Washo values often conflict with white values. Unfortunately, the Washo are, in the final analysis, dependent on the white world.

The Future

The nature of the Washo future will be determined by the processes of the Washo past. From the earliest contact between whites and Washo, the Washo have made adjustments to a changed situation. The whites in many cases were a new resource to be exploited to the benefit of the Washo. Many of the changes in Washo life were sought eagerly because they provided an easier and more profitable access to food and desirable materials. The pattern of wandering bands continued from the 1840s until the 1920s for some families. Hunting and gathering in the Washo environment required a flexible social structure and cultural patterns permitting the individual the widest latitude in seeking subsistence. The Washo response to the changes of the past century have been in keeping with this pattern. It has been opportunistic and flexible with the widest range of individual responses. The individual Washo and his family has made adjustments to the new situation as best suited him and served his purposes. Because of this pattern of change, the Washo have become increasingly involved with the white society and the future of the Washo people is linked to the future of America in general. Patterns of deprivation, racial discrimination, and education will determine the future of the Washo.

References Used

Direct citations are few in the text itself, but the author has frequently used information drawn from the following works:

ANGEL, MYRON (ed.), 1958. Reproduction of Thompson and West's *History of Nevada,* 1881. (Originally published by T. H. Thompson and Albert A. West, 1881, reproduced by Howell-North, Berkeley, 1958).

COOK, SHERBORNE, F., 1941, "The Mechanisms and Extent of Dietary Change among Certain Groups of California and Nevada Indians," *Ibero-Americana,* Vol. 18, pp. 1–59.

D'AZAVEDO, WARREN L. (ed.), 1963, "The Washo Indians of California and Nevada," University of Utah, Department of Anthropology, Anthropological Papers, No. 67, August. (Contains articles by S. A. Barrett, W. L. d'Azavedo, S. A. Freed, R. S. Freed, P. E. Leis, N. A. Scotch, F. L. Scotch, J. A. Price, and J. F. Downs).

DOWNS, JAMES F., 1961, "Washo Religion," University of California *Anthropological Record,* Vol. 14, No. 6, pp. 349–418.

INGALLS, G. W., 1913, "Indians of Nevada, 1825 to 1931," in Sam P. Davis, (ed.), *The History of Nevada,* pp. 239–69.

LOWIE, ROBERT H., 1939, "Ethnographic Notes on the Washo," University of California Publications in American Archaeology and Ethnology. Vol. 36, No. 5, pp. 301–52.

PRICE, JOHN A., 1962, "Washo Economy," Nevada State Museum Anthropological Papers, No. 6.

———, 1962, "Washo Economy," unpublished M.A. thesis, Department of Anthropology, University of Utah.

STEWART, OMER G., 1941, "Culture Element Distributions: XIV, Northern Paiute," University of California *Anthropological Record,* Vol. 4, No. 3, pp. 361–446.

———, 1944, "Washo-Northern Paiute Peyotism: A Study in Acculturation," University of California Publications in American Archaeology and Ethnology, Vol. 40, No. 3, pp. 63–142.

Recommended Reading

DRIVER, HAROLD E., 1961, *Indians of North America*. Chicago: University of Chicago Press.

A general reference work outlining the results of many years of research by many anthropologists in the collection of data on the distribution of culture traits. It includes information on many categories of culture for the several major culture areas of native North America.

KROEBER, ALFRED A., 1925, *Handbook of the Indians of California*. Bureau of American Ethnology Bulletin No. 78 (reprinted by the California Book Company, Berkeley, 1953).

A major compendium of information on the culture, language, social organization, and material culture of the tribes of California by the leading authority on the area.

———, 1948, "Cultural and Natural Areas of Native North America," University of California Publications in American Archaeology and Ethnology, Vol. 38, pp. 1–242.

An examination of the relationship between culture and environment among the Indian tribes of the United States and Canada.

LA BARRE, WESTON, 1938, *The Peyote Cult*. New Haven, Conn.: Yale University Publications in Anthropology.

A discussion of the history and dynamics of the peyote religion.

SPENCER, ROBERT F., AND JENNINGS, JESSE D., 1964, *The Native Americans*. New York: Harper & Row.

An excellent general treatment of the prehistory and ethnography of the American Indian prepared by a number of experts in the various culture areas of Mexico, the United States, and Canada, with ethnographic sketchs of representative tribes.

STEWART, JULIAN H. 1938, *Basin-Plateau Socio-Political Groups,* Washington, D.C.: Bureau of American Ethnology Bulletin 120.

A classic work describing the culture, social organization, and economic life of the peoples of the Great Basin.